FAITH AND CRITICISM

Faith and Criticism

The Sarum Lectures 1992

BASIL MITCHELL

CLARENDON PRESS · OXFORD
1994

Oxford University Press, Walton Street, Oxford OX2 6DP
Oxford New York Toronto
Delhi Bombay Calcutta Madras Karachi
Kuala Lumpur Singapore Hong Kong Tokyo
Nairobi Dar es Salaam Cape Town
Melbourne Auckland Madrid
and associated companies in
Berlin Ibadan

Oxford is a trade mark of Oxford University Press

Published in the United States
by Oxford University Press Inc., New York

British Library Cataloguing in Publication Data
Data available

Library of Congress Cataloging in Publication Data
Faith and criticism/Basil Mitchell.
(The Sarum lectures; 1992)
1. Faith and reason—Christianity. 2. Modernist—fundamentalist
controversy. I. Title. II. Series.
BT50.M56 1994   231'.042—dc20   94–16380
ISBN 0–19–826758–4

1 3 5 7 9 10 8 6 4 2

Typeset by Cambrian Typesetters Frimley, Surrey
Printed in Great Britain
on acid-free paper by
Biddles Ltd., Guildford and King's Lynn

To J. R. L.

PREFACE

This book comprises the Sarum Lectures given at the University of Oxford in 1992, largely as they were delivered. They derive from a decade of reflection on the nature of faith and its relationship to rational criticism. My thinking on the subject was greatly assisted by the opportunity of giving the Nathaniel Taylor Lectures at Yale University and the Norton Lectures at Southern Baptist Seminary, in 1985 and 1989, for which I am most grateful.

The more I reflected on the question as it relates to individuals, the more I became convinced of its relevance to controversial issues in morality, education, and politics which are treated in the final three chapters of this book.

I am grateful to John Lucas for consistent encouragement and criticism, and to Michael Banner for his care in reading and commenting on the text. Among those who helped with individual chapters were William J. Abraham, Jean Porter, Jill Rattle, and Robert Mermagen.

A special debt of gratitude is owed to Jenny Wagstaffe who in all the stages of preparing the lectures enabled me to enjoy the benefits of computer technology without having to master it myself.

Basil Mitchell

CONTENTS

I

Faith and Criticism:
A Problem for Theology

It has often been remarked that the most striking disagreements nowadays in matters of theology are to be found not between the denominations but within them. They cut entirely across denominational boundaries. In particular, within all the mainstream churches there is a sharp division between those who take it for granted that Christian theology should be studied critically with the aid of all the resources of modern scholarship and with due attention to all that is received as knowledge in the modern world, and those who resist this trend as destructive of the historic faith of Christians. Let us call them liberals and conservatives. I am aware of the dangers of marking the distinction I wish to make by the use of these expressions. 'Liberal theology' in particular has all sorts of associations in the history of theology which are not related to the sense I wish to give the term, but I could not find any other pair of opposites which would convey unambiguously the distinction I have in mind. So I intend a purely stipulative definition of these terms. For the purpose of this book they mean just what I want them to mean and nothing else.

Conservatives and liberals, as I am defining them, have one, substantial assumption in common. They both take it for granted that Christianity has a truth to impart about the world and man's place in it in the light of which salvation is to be understood. This may seem so obvious as to be scarcely worth mentioning, but in relation to some recent developments in theology it becomes significant. Indeed, the fact that they share this assumption may make both parties, together with my taking pains to distinguish between them, seem somewhat old-fashioned.

It is this very concern with the truth about things which sets the agenda for liberal theology. The problem, as liberals see it, is that we have available to us sources of knowledge which are independent of the Christian tradition and which, since truth is one, need to be in some way brought into relation with it. Theologians must, to take the most obvious examples, take full account of the Darwinian theory of natural selection in endeavouring to understand creation and they must take seriously the findings of the literary and historical study of the Bible and of Christian origins in interpreting revelation. By contrast, conservatives—as I am defining them—take their stand upon the Christian tradition, whether represented by the Bible or the authority of the Church, and are prepared if need be to reject the claims of modern knowledge altogether if they conflict with it. The concern which preoccupies the liberals does not present itself to them as a problem (although it may, of course, exert an influence upon them in various other ways).

In working out the liberal programme there is

inevitably a tension between those whose primary concern is to safeguard the tradition—to ensure that no element of truth in it is lost—and those who want above all to do full justice to modern discoveries and contemporary experience. We may call them 'traditionalists' and 'progressives'. (We often use the terms 'conservatives' and 'liberals' to make this distinction too, and I may later do so myself when there is no risk of confusion.) It will be one of my main contentions that this tension is not only unavoidable but entirely desirable in theology as in any other intellectual pursuit. Progressives will often be critical of the tradition, alert to the presence of elements in it which are not essential to the faith. Traditionalists will often be suspicious of what passes as 'modern knowledge' and determined not to assimilate Christianity to the prevailing secular world view. Left to the traditionalists alone the tradition tends to ossify. In the hands of the progressives alone it is liable to become dissolved in the secular culture.

But that is for later. In the present chapter and the two following ones, I intend to examine one central argument against liberal theology. It is an argument which, I believe, has a good deal of substance in it, and provides much of the attraction which fundamentalism exerts upon genuinely Christian minds. It also, as we shall see later, inspires some strongly radical ventures in theology. In the course of rebutting this argument I shall develop a positive account of the relationship between faith and criticism in Christian theology.

After a review in Chapter 4 of the historical background to the problem I shall in Chapter 5 vindicate my solution against the assaults of post-modernism and in so doing justify my conviction that there is a problem in need of solution. It may seem surprising that I should leave it until half-way through the book to consider a fashionable objection to my whole way of proceeding. My reason is this: if it is being maintained that a problem which seems to arise does not in fact arise, an effective—perhaps the most effective—reply to the objection is to engage in intelligible and persuasive discourse on the basis that it does arise. In the last three chapters I shall explore the implications of what has been said for morality, religious education, and relations between Church and State.

The criticism of liberal theology I have in mind runs as follows: Christian faith is unconditional. It demands our complete and whole-hearted allegiance. But to allow Christian belief to be exposed to criticism implies that criticism might turn out to be fatal. Once it is allowed that faith is, in principle, vulnerable to criticism, its character is bound to change. In place of the total commitment which is demanded of Christians we have a faith which is tentative and provisional. If we take reason as our advocate, reason will demand to be judge, and in that court faith will constantly be at risk.

This is a criticism which, it seems to me, liberal theologians cannot dismiss as if it need not concern them. For it presents a problem which arises within liberal theology itself. Liberal theologians cannot accept with equanimity the charge that, as defenders of the faith, they lack conviction; and the charge is all the more serious if it follows not merely from personal or institutional weakness, which might be remedied, but from an inherent flaw in their entire approach.

In giving as the title to this book *Faith and Criticism*, it is this problem, then, that I wish to address. The issue has been posed in a characteristically forceful way by Professor D. Z. Phillips in his book *Faith after Foundationalism*,[1] in which he gets some pleasing entertainment out of my own views about the place of reason in religion. In *The Justification of Religious Belief* I argued that conclusions in matters of religion are typically arrived at by a process of cumulative argument developed in an essentially informal way. Phillips speculates how, holding these views, I might recite the 139th Psalm, which runs in the Authorized Version:

> Whither shall I go from thy spirit?
> or whither shall I flee from thy presence?
> If I ascend up into heaven, thou art there;
> If I make my bed in hell, behold thou art there.
> If I take the wings of the morning,
> And dwell in the uttermost parts of the sea;
> Even there shall thy hand lead me,
> And thy right hand shall hold me.

Mitchell, says Phillips, will have to say:

> If I ascend into heaven, thou art probably there;
> If I make my bed in hell, it is cumulatively likely
>   that thou art there,

and so on.

He notes the confidence of the psalmist's language and comments that 'it never occurred to any prophet or

---

[1] (London: Routledge, 1988), 9–10.

writer in the Old Testament to seek evidence for the existence of God, let alone to prove it'. That is to say, the psalmist, in his superb poem, speaks with the accents of complete conviction, and commits himself utterly to the providence of God: whereas the liberal thinker, conscious of the tentative and provisional character of all our beliefs, can only manage a carefully qualified assent.

Mention of Phillips suggests a further reason why the problem of faith and criticism should be considered as a problem within the practice of liberal theology. For to regard it simply as an issue between conservatives and liberals would be to overlook the fact that critics of liberalism are by no means all conservative Christians who hold to the literal truth of Holy Scripture. Phillips himself is not. Following the philosophy of Wittgenstein and deeply influenced by religious thinkers like Kierke-gaard and Simone Weil, he regards the sphere of truth and meaning in religion as simply incommensurable with the facts of science and common sense. He could not say, with the Creationists, that the Darwinian theory of evolution is false, because it conflicts with truths revealed in Genesis. This would be to presuppose that the Christian doctrine of Creation and the Darwinian theory of evolution can come into conflict, so that one or other of them must be rejected. Rather he holds that the meaning and truth of religious claims are to be found wholly within religion itself. As Wittgenstein put it, the religious 'language-game' is to be understood in its own terms in relation to its own appropriate 'form of life'. Hence it is a fundamental error to suppose that religious utterances, when properly understood, can be exposed to scientific or historical criticism or require the support of scientific or historical evidence.

What Phillips and the conservatives have in common is a conviction that Christianity is true and all-important and that its truth is in principle impregnable against rational criticism. They agree in holding that to admit the propriety of rational criticism would be to deprive religious faith of that unconditional commitment which is its hallmark. But, whereas the conservatives insist that what is said in Holy Scripture is literally true so that any scientific or historical judgements which conflict with it must be false, Phillips defines religious truth in such a way that it cannot, as a matter of logic, come into conflict with these other truths, whose proper domain is outside the religious language-game altogether.

Phillips is by no means alone in his radical critique of liberal theology. The existentialist philosophy of Rudolf Bultmann, itself deeply influenced by Kierkegaard, exhibits essentially the same pattern of reasoning. Faith, Bultmann argues, is a matter of unconditional commitment to Christ, but such commitment could not conceivably be justified if it rested on any logical or historical grounds. Therefore it does not rest on such grounds, but is wholly a matter of radical existential choice. As he puts it:

Thus it is impossible to prove that faith is related to its object. But . . . it is just here that its strength lies. For if it were susceptible to proof it would mean that we could know and establish God apart from faith, and that would be placing him on a level with the world of tangible objective reality.[2]

---

[2] 'A Reply to the Theses of S. Schniewind', in Hans Werner Bartsch (ed.), *Kerygma and Myth* (London: SPCK, 1953), 103–4.

Bultmann and his followers have been overtaken by even more radical thinkers, generally known collectively as 'post-modernists', whose views I shall consider later (chiefly in Chapter 5). They represent a further and more extreme reaction to the challenge of science and the 'scientific world-view'. Bultmann and Phillips take the scientific world-view as entirely mandatory for us today, so that we cannot accept or even understand any would-be factual claims that conflict with it. Accordingly, the truth of religion must be of a different order from the truth of science and common sense, so that they are not in competition with one another. These later thinkers, following clues in Nietzsche, go one step further and abandon the concept of objective truth altogether. They hold that science itself has no better claim than any other set of beliefs to tell us how the world is. Its role is purely pragmatic. The implications for the problem I am concerned with are similar to those that follow from the views of Bultmann and Phillips. There can be no problem of faith and criticism, since the scientific discoveries and scholarly research which provide the basis for criticism are no more secure than Christian faith itself.

The variety of theological positions which appeal to the primacy of unconditional commitment is remarkable and affords the liberal a base for counter-attack. Since the primacy of unconditional commitment is compatible with, on the one hand, extreme biblical fundamentalism and, on the other, radical existentialism, not to mention the varieties of post-modernism, how, the believer may ask, is he to choose between these alternatives? He could do so by considering how each of them stands in relation to the witness of scripture, the tradition of the Church, accumulated experience of Christians and the sum of human knowledge. But this would be to attempt a rational assessment of the sort that all the parties mentioned are agreed in rejecting.

As an *argumentum ad hominem* this rejoinder is effective. The strongest single objection to biblical fundamentalism and radical existentialism alike is that neither, on its own terms, can afford any reason why one should choose it rather than some other alternative. The post-modernists cannot even intelligibly raise the question. Why be a Christian and not an Islamic fundamentalist? Why exercise one's radical freedom of choice in favour of Christ rather than Mohammed, or, indeed, Nietzsche? But it is not enough simply to pursue this dialectical advantage if one has no adequate reply to the insistent challenge which these various parties present to the whole programme of liberal theology. It may be that their own positions suffer from an ineradicable weakness, but it may yet be the case that the liberal's is fatally flawed too. It is a mistake common in theological controversy to suppose that in relation to any question there are only two possible answers, which are mutually exclusive and together exhaust the field.

I am assuming, then, for the purpose of this book that liberal theologians must take seriously the challenge to their programme from insistence upon the unconditional nature of faith. They cannot deny that the New Testament writers, like the prophets before them and the Fathers after them, speak with the accents of firm conviction. If it is the case, as the opponents of liberalism allege, that such conviction is incompatible with the role the liberal feels compelled to allow to rational criticism, it must, at the very least, call in question the liberal's claim to stand in the direct line of authentic Christianity. And not only that. Faith is not only a theological virtue; it is a moral virtue too. Where faith is weak or equivocal or merely tentative it cannot withstand the tests to which in extremity it may be exposed or even the less dramatic pressures of 'the common round, the daily task'.

This last consideration suggests a way we might proceed. Religious faith is often discussed as if it were something altogether different from any attitude encountered in non-religious contexts. To talk of faith as a 'theological virtue' is already to suggest this. It is a commonplace to contrast the committed nature of religious faith with the scientist's freedom from bias and willingness at all times to be guided by the evidence alone. It is partly for this reason, indeed, that the readiness of the liberal academic theologian to attend to the findings and the arguments of scientists and historical and linguistic scholars is itself interpreted by conservatives as a surrender to secular values. Open-mindedness is thought to be an essentially secular attribute to be contrasted with the unquestioning commitment which characterizes religious faith.

I want to consider in the remainder of this chapter and in part of the next how far this popular contrast is justified. My claim will be that faith, far from being the antithesis of rationality, is an essential requirement of any kind of effective intellectual endeavour.

The conception of reason presupposed by the familiar contrast between reason and faith is made explicit in the

well-known statement by W. K. Clifford: 'It is wrong, always, everywhere and for everyone to believe anything upon insufficient evidence.'[3] It follows that, in order to be rational, one must:
— have sufficient evidence for what one believes
— be prepared to produce the evidence on demand
— proportion one's confidence in the truth of the belief to the evidence as it stands at the time of speaking.

In all matters of any importance, in relation to one's moral, political or religious convictions, for example, the evidence is inevitably subtle, complex, and variable over time. Hence, it will not normally be possible, if one sticks to Clifford's dictum, to hold such beliefs in other than a tentative and provisional manner. Frequently, the only proper thing to do will be to suspend judgement. The paradigm case of the unprejudiced thinker is the scientist, who is entirely open-minded and accepts or rejects a hypothesis on the basis of the experimental evidence alone.

We are so used to this conception of reason that we often fail to notice how remote it is from the way people actually think. No-one was more aware of this or criticized it more effectively than John Henry Newman. Newman had encountered it in Locke and commented: 'He (Locke) consults his own ideal of how the mind ought to act, instead of investigating human nature as an existing thing, or as it is found in the world.'[4] When he examined the way we actually think, Newman noticed a number of things:

[3] *Lectures and Essays* (London: Macmillan, 1886), 346.
[4] *An Essay in Aid of a Grammar of Assent* (London: Longmans, 1890), 164.

(*a*) Much of our reasoning is tacit and informal. It cannot be neatly displayed as a set of conclusions derived by a straightforward process of inference from clear-cut premises. Rather: 'It is the cumulation of probabilities, independent of each other, arising out of the nature and circumstances of the particular case which is under review; probabilities too fine to avail separately, too subtle and circuitous to be convertible into syllogisms, too numerous and various for such conversion, even were they convertible.'[5]

(*b*) Thus, most arguments are cumulative in form. A wide range of considerations of very varied character is involved. No one of them suffices to generate the required conclusion, but, taken together, they may converge irresistibly upon it. Newman illustrates his contention with examples taken from everyday life:

Let a person only call to mind the clear impression he has about matters of every day's ocurrence, that this man is bent on a certain object, or that that man was displeased, or another suspicious; or that that one is happy, and another unhappy; and how much depends in such impressions on manner, voice, accent, words offered, silence instead of words, and all the many symptoms which are felt by the mind, but cannot be contemplated; and let him consider how very poor account he is able to give of his impression, if he avows it and is called upon to justify it. This, indeed, is meant by what is called moral proof, in opposition to legal.[6]

Some of the best examples are to be found in novels. One of my favourites is the passage in Jane Austen's

[5] *An Essay in Aid of a Grammar of Assent*, 288.
[6] Newman, in Mackinnon and Holmes (eds.), *University Sermons*, (London: SPCK, 1970), 274.

Emma in which Emma discusses with Mr John Knightley, her brother-in-law, the attitude to her of the clergyman Mr Elton, and dismisses with indignation the suggestion that he is in love with her. Emma remarks:

'There is such pefect good temper and good will in Mr Elton as one cannot but value.'

'Yes', said Mr John Knightley presently, with some slyness, 'he seems to have a great deal of good-will towards *you*.'

'Me', she replied with a smile of astonishment, 'are you imagining me to be Mr Elton's object?'

'Such an imagination has crossed me, I own, Emma; and if it never occurred to you before, you may as well take it into consideration now.'

'Mr Elton in love with me! — What an idea!'

'I do not say it is so, but you will do well to consider whether it is so, or not, and to regulate your behaviour accordingly. I think your manner to him encouraging. I speak as a friend, Emma. You had better look about you, and ascertain what you do, and what you mean to do.'

'I thank you, but I assure you you are quite mistaken. Mr Elton and I are very good friends, and nothing more;' and she walked on, amusing herself in the consideration of the blunders which often arise from the partial knowledge of circumstance, of the mistakes which people of high pretension to judgement are for ever falling into; and not very well pleased with her brother for imagining her blind and ignorant, and in want of counsel.[7]

There is a delightful irony in this. Emma wilfully misreads all the signs which seem so clear to Mr John Knightley who, as the reader knows, is in the right. Yet

[7] *Emma*, ed. Ronald Blythe (Harmondsworth: Penguin Books, 1966), 133–4.

there is quite obviously no satisfactory way of formalizing the argument on either side.

(c) In estimating the force of the evidence and in deciding what is to be believed on the strength of it we are rightly influenced by considerations other than those provided by the evidence itself. We bring to the evidence antecedent assumptions which inevitably, and Newman thinks rightly, affect our interpretation of it. It is simply not the case that we approach the evidence, whatever it may be, with a totally open mind. At the very least we bring to bear upon it the concepts embedded in the language we use, but also a host of beliefs about things and people, about associations and institutions which we may not be fully aware of and, even if we were, could not clearly and fully articulate. This accounts for the enormous difficulty we sometimes experience in debating contentious issues with people who differ in principle from ourselves. It is not that they are, in any obvious way, less rational or less observant than we are, but, as we often say, they 'see things differently'. This often becomes particularly apparent in televised debates. People are at cross-purposes with one another, and if there is a presenter, he or she generally makes things worse. Instead of helping to trace the different assumptions of the disputants, and teasing out the variations in vocabulary, the presenter tries to reduce it all to some common formula which, it is supposed, we simple viewers will understand, and which inevitably misrepresents the positions of both the contending parties.

The expression 'antecedent assumptions' covers a range of things. Most straightforwardly, it includes theories or whole systems of thought which a particular individual takes for granted. It was interesting to observe the very different judgements upon the causes and development of the French Revolution, evoked by the bicentenary celebrations in France. The events look very different to liberal and to Marxist historians; different again to conservative anti-Jacobins. There is, of course, a sense in which they agree as to the evidence—that a mob stormed the Bastille, for example, on 14 July 1789 and found seven prisoners there, and innumerable comparable facts—but they differ profoundly as to what it is reasonable to believe on the basis of these facts. Moreover, as Newman uses the expression 'antecedent assumptions', it also includes the personality and even the moral character of the individual who makes the judgement. As Newman puts it: 'though a given evidence does not vary in force, the antecedent probability attending it does vary without limit, according to the temper of the mind surveying it.'[8] That this is so is, perhaps, most evident in the case of those persons whose primary duty it is to free their minds from every kind of bias, namely judges. Two judges may be faced by the same evidence and be guided by the same precedents and statutes or—in the case of justices of the US Supreme Court—the same provisions of the Constitution, and yet come to different conclusions without there necessarily being any suggestion of bias or other impropriety.

(d) What we have said so far, following Newman, about the ways in which people actually think, about what constitutes 'rationality' in ordinary life, leads

---

[8] *University Sermons*, 193.

naturally to a fourth consideration which bears more closely on the relevance of faith. If our appreciation of evidence and our assessment of the conclusions that follow from it is generally tacit and implicit, and if the process of reasoning is conducted within a framework of assumptions which are to some extent influenced by the individual's entire character and personality, a certain stability over time in these assumptions is necessary. Clifford's dictum would require that any change in the weight of evidence for a system of belief should immediately be reflected in some modification of the system or some variation in the confidence reposed in it. But this manifestly does not happen. People hold on to their beliefs when things get difficult and must do so if they are to be properly developed and tested.

This feature of our large-scale beliefs is so important that it needs to be explored in greater depth. We must notice, first of all, that it applies even in the case of scientific systems which are thought to provide the very paradigm of open-mindedness. Clifford's dictum is appropriate only to what T. S. Kuhn[9] calls 'normal science', in which the researcher is trying to test a hypothesis within the framework of a well-developed branch of the subject. In such a case the fundamental laws and central concepts of that branch of science are not in dispute or at all at risk from the outcome of the experiment. The researcher is entirely open-minded as to the truth of the hypothesis and will accept or reject it according as the experiment falls out. If the results of the experiment are inconclusive the researcher will have only

---

[9] *Structure of Scientific Revolutions* (Chicago, 1962), passim.

such confidence in the hypothesis as the evidence
warrants; if they are equivocal he or she will suspend
judgement. This is because the antecedent assumptions
are held steady throughout the proceedings and are not
themselves called in question. The situation is quite
different when more fundamental scientific laws or
concepts are at issue. It was Kuhn's peculiar contribution
to the history and philosophy of science to recognize
that 'scientific revolutions' occur in the course of which
the issue at stake is precisely what organizing concepts
should be employed and what basic laws acknowledged.
Kuhn has been criticized, rightly so far as I can judge,
for exaggerating the difference between normal and
revolutionary science, but his significance for our
purposes is not affected by this. What we learn from him
is that, in so far as fresh discoveries threaten the received
scientific picture, it is simply not the case that the
essential features of the system are at once abandoned or
confidence in them allowed to fluctuate from day to
day. A variety of devices is resorted to in order to avoid
such a consequence. Comparatively low-level theories
are jettisoned or modified in order to accommodate the
new observations; sometimes the observations themselves are questioned; or the episode is placed in
parenthesis, as it were, as an as yet unsolved problem.
As Kuhn puts it epigrammatically: 'If any and every
failure to fit were ground for theory rejection, all
theories ought to be rejected at all times.'[10] The
'puzzles' that 'normal science' attempts to solve are set
precisely by the occurrence of observations that are

[10] Ibid. 146–7.

incompatible with the findings of science as they now stand.

Meanwhile the existing overall structure is retained until there is available an alternative system which is better able to account for all the evidence and which, in turn, is able to generate programmes of research which will, of course, then be confronted by their own puzzles.

Hence, scientists operate what has been called a 'principle of tenacity', in virtue of which they do not let go of their fundamental beliefs when things get difficult, but rather persevere in the hope, or—shall we say?—the faith, that the problem will eventually be resolved. Their characteristic attitude is well expressed by Darwin in the concluding sentences of *The Origin of Species*: 'A crowd of difficulties will have occurred to the reader. Some of them are so grave that to this day I can never reflect on them without being staggered; but, to the best of my judgement, the greater number are only apparent; and those that are real are not, I think, fatal to my theory.'[11] Two things are to be noticed here. One is that Darwin does not at all minimize the difficulties. He is, in that sense, open-minded and impartial. The other is that, in spite of fully acknowledging them, he continues to trust his theory. And it is apparent, I think, that both these attitudes are essential to scientific progress. Without an honest appreciation of the difficulties, the theory would never get tested and developed. Without the determination to soldier on in the face of difficulties the process of testing and development would never have time to operate effectively.

[11] Quoted in Michael Banner, *The Justification of Science and the Rationality of Religious Belief* (Oxford University Press, 1990), 182.

In the light of this discussion it becomes apparent that the contrast which is often drawn, not least by theologians, between the entirely open-minded approach of the scientist and the committed nature of religious faith is, at the very least, overdrawn. Nevertheless, it would be a mistake to pretend that there are no differences at all. The chief differences are, I suggest:

(*a*) that, in the natural sciences, at any rate, at any given time, the preponderance of evidence in favour of a particular complex of theories is likely to be so marked as to make it plainly sensible to persevere with it in the face of temporary difficulties;

(*b*) that, even when this is not so, the pragmatic advantages of a degree of tenacity are fairly obvious. Where scientists differ, and both cannot be right, the truth is more likely to emerge if both parties adhere pretty stubbornly to their own hypotheses, so that they can be fully tested against one another. In other words, 'faith' (if this is the right word to use) is such an obvious requirement of scientific procedures that, in this connection, there is no place for a 'problem of faith and reason'. Nevertheless we need to realize that such disagreements can be very persistent. Since the 1930s there has been a deep division among physicists about how to interpret the fundamental concepts of quantum mechanics. Each side in the dispute holds to its opinion, though well aware of the criticisms offered by the other.

But the sciences do not exhaust the whole of our intellectual life and the natural sciences do not exhaust the whole of science. If I am to establish my contention that the problem of the relationship between faith and criticism is not confined to theology but is characteristic, in varying degrees of intensity, of all serious intellectual endeavours, I shall need to go beyond the natural sciences into the social sciences, the humanities, and overall philosophies of life. And that will be the subject of the next chapter.

2

Faith and Criticism:
The Problem Generalized

In the first chapter I set out the problems which I want
to investigate and which, as I think, lie at the heart of the
liberal approach to theology. A liberal, in the sense I am
giving to the term, is one who acknowledges an
obligation to expose the Christian faith to criticism in
the light of modern knowledge, whether that derives
from the natural sciences, the historical and linguistic
study of the Bible, or any other branch of study that can
be shown to be relevant. The problem, as critics of
liberalism see it, is that any such acknowledgement is
incompatible with the unconditional commitment which
is inseparable from authentic Christian faith. The critics
in question are, most conspicuously, fundamentalists
who base their criticism upon the inerrancy of the Holy
Scripture, but essentially the same challenge to liberalism
is forthcoming from an entirely different direction—that
of more radical theologies. What is denied, in both
instances, is that Christian beliefs could, even in
principle, be rejected or modified because they cannot
be squared with modern knowledge. Fundamentalists
admit that Christian beliefs can conflict with 'modern

knowledge' and hold that, where this happens, the claims of 'modern knowledge' should be repudiated. Radicals deny that such conflicts are possible, so long as the nature of Christian faith is properly understood.

The contention that openness to criticism is incompatible with commitment derives from a certain familiar conception of the way reason works, which associates reason with complete open-mindedness and a readiness at every moment to be swayed entirely by the state of the evidence as it appears at that time. It is the conception represented by W. K. Clifford's celebrated dictum.[1] The inadequacies of this view are exposed by Newman, who notes that in all matters of importance we tend to hold on to our central beliefs despite fluctuations in the state of the evidence. That this is so is apparent even in the very case where faith of any kind is generally thought to be out of place, namely that of science, at least when important principles are at stake. And as one moves from the natural sciences, through the biological to the psychological and social sciences and on to the humanities, the role of faith becomes steadily more apparent. When one advances further still from academic pursuits of any kind to what one may call 'world-views' or 'philosophies of life' the significance of faith becomes even more marked.

One can distinguish two stages in this further progress:

The first is that of the human sciences and the humanities. It is characteristic of these that they are fields of greater or less controversy. 'Schools of thought'

---

[1] Quoted on p. 11.

make their appearance and their adherents fight it out in the academic arena. Sometimes the battle lines are drawn up between disciplines, sometimes within them. Examples are the continuing debate between nature and nurture in the social sciences or between behaviourism and mentalism in psychology, or the claims of socio- biology in relation to sociology. Consider also the vogue for quantitative methods in history as against insistence on the central role of empathy or *verstehen*.

People who are not themselves academics sometimes like to believe that open-mindedness is the characteristic virtue of academics and that their possession of this virtue is one of the things that separates them in their 'ivory tower' from the hurly-burly of the real world outside. No-one with any actual experience of academic life could retain this notion for a moment. Scholars are, as a rule, deeply committed to one among a number of possible approaches to their subject, and, in conse- quence, partiality and prejudice are vices constantly to be guarded against.

But am I not, in effect, making a case for partiality and prejudice, in arguing the need for something akin to faith in academic life? Prejudice, in a sense, yes, but partiality no. Impartiality is a fundamental academic virtue. It requires one to be scrupulous in assembling the evidence, honest in recognizing arguments against one's position, fair in assessing the force of these arguments, sympathetic in representing the position of those with whom one disagrees. Academics all too often fail to satisfy these requirements, but failure nevertheless it is, and the requirements are absolute.

The mistake lies in supposing that one cannot exhibit

the virtue of impartiality while holding fast to firm
convictions of one's own. Impartiality does not imply
neutrality. If it did, we should indeed be in a hopeless
case. We should have to choose between firm convictions
and fairness in debate. It is, I think, impossible to
exaggerate the effects in our contemporary culture of
the mistaken assumption that firm commitment is
incompatible with honest recognition of difficulties.
There is a moving passage in Robert Bellah's *Habits of
the Heart* in which he and his collaborators remark
about many younger people: 'They long for the unquestioning commitment their parents seemed to have,
yet they are repelled by what they take to be the lack of
communication, the repression of difficulties, and,
indeed, the resigned fatalism such commitment seems to
imply. These respondents both envy their parents and
resolve never to be like them.'² That firm conviction
involves the repression of difficulties is an assumption
shared by both sides in this sad inter-generational
impasse. That it is a false assumption is evident from the
example of Darwin. He is aware of difficulties in his
theory and appreciates their force, but he remains
convinced of its truth.

Neutrality is to be distinguished from impartiality and
is not implied by it. Impartiality requires not that I
refrain from reaching a conclusion about a disputed
question, or communicating that conclusion to others,
but that I am fair to the arguments of my opponents;
that I do not misrepresent them or underestimate their
weight. Hence the concept of impartiality, as distinct

---

² (University of California Press, 1985), 103.

from neutrality, has its place only in debates where rational standards of argument apply.

To say that the human sciences and the humanities are inherently controversial is to recognize that, although a given position may in fact be rationally preferable to its rivals, this is rarely obvious. The points that Newman notices, and to which I referred in my first chapter, go far to explain why this is so. The issues in dispute are complex, highly ramified, and calling for trained judgement and sympathetic imagination. The resolution of any individual problem can rarely be achieved simply by inspecting the evidence provided by the present case. There will always be an immense background of theory, related to earlier observations, which cannot in practice be made wholly explicit, but which guides the thinking of the disputants. Although there may be hidden inconsistencies, these systems of thought generally possess a massive coherence, in virtue of which it would be unreasonable to abandon them readily, or even modify them radically, in the face of difficulties. It is, in any case, possible to make sense of fresh experience only if one is equipped with a conceptual scheme adequate to the task. The point is beautifully illustrated by Edith Wharton, when she remarks of one of her less sophisticated characters, a rich American lady who is making a world tour, 'Unprepared as she was for the sights awaiting her, she has necessarily observed little, and understood less'.

I have assumed so far that the interest of academics in their subject is purely theoretical, so that the strategies appropriate to their task are those required just for the extension of knowledge, but very often this is not the case. In so far as the human sciences form the basis for the actual practice of, for example, medicine or social work, it is necessary to decide which of the (more or less) disputed theories is to be presupposed. To take a particular example, the theories of Piaget about cognitive development have influenced an entire generation of educational theorists and so of educational practitioners. They have reinforced the influence of Dewey and others in favour of allowing the child to determine his or her rate of progress and militated against the imposition of formal structures whether of learning or testing. This approach to education has become strongly entrenched in colleges of education and centres of educational administration. It is possible—especially when such an educational fashion is coming to an end—to criticize the willingness of many highly intelligent people to follow the trend unhesitatingly. And yet something of the sort was bound to happen, given the imperatives of practical choice. Unless the findings of the human sciences are to be entirely ignored a choice has to be made in practice between competing theories and, once the choice has been made, a massive orthodoxy is almost bound to develop, whose institutional embodiment it will be very hard for individuals to resist. Whereas, in a purely theoretical endeavour, it is comparatively easy and appropriate to suspend judgement (although only, as we have seen, within limits), this is not possible when large scale decisions have to be made involving numerous individuals and complex institutions.

We can now see how (as Newman notices) the personalities of the individuals concerned are also affected. By contrast with the older authoritarian pattern of schoolteacher, providing instruction from a secure basis of received values, the newer teacher is flexible and non-judgemental, as befits the newer theories. The sort of person one is, is itself profoundly affected by the character of one's basic convictions.

It is evident, therefore, that if these convictions are to change radically, it will not, as a rule, be due to this or that particular piece of evidence, or this or that fresh experience, but as a result of a steady accumulation of considerations which together persuade the individual that his or her existing mind-set is no longer adequate and requires either to be drastically revised or abandoned altogether. And this process of change cannot be purely intellectual, because strong emotions and entrenched habits are involved. There are also loyalties to like-minded colleagues and, perhaps, professional associations, to be taken into account. These things are partly, but by no means wholly, non-rational. If it matters to be guided by true principles, it matters that they should be generally acknowledged and widely influential. One ought not, then, by individual action, to weaken their effectiveness, whenever doubts occur to one, but only when the case against them has become very clear, which will normally be only when the claims of some alternative scheme of thought have been established beyond reasonable doubt.

If this is true of academic subjects when they have practical applications, it is even more obviously true of world-views or philosophies of life, which comprise the second stage. For these are not only practical, but also comprehensive. They afford a 'faith to live by' and they claim, in principle, to embrace the whole of our experience. There is, indeed, an overlap between them and the academic disciplines we have just been considering. Any philosophy of life, in view of its claims to comprehensiveness, will need to take account of the various branches of knowledge (even, if only, like fundamentalism, to dispute their claims); and the latter will make their own characteristic contribution to philosophies of life. Thus, for example, the philosophy of life advanced by B. F. Skinner in his *Beyond Freedom and Dignity*[3] is largely based upon the behaviourist interpretation of human personality which he adopts as an academic psychologist. And the educational theories associated with Dewey and Piaget have a natural affinity with a broad type of liberal humanism. It is very common, in fact, for academics, particularly those who are at home in the human sciences, to venture into metaphysics without realizing that this is what they are doing, and to claim scientific authority illicitly for their philosophical speculations.

Now that we have arrived at the consideration of world-views or philosophies of life, we need to recognize explicitly a distinction which has only been implicit so far. We need to distinguish between the role of faith in the pursuit of truth and its role in the search for liberation or salvation.

(a) The pursuit of fuller truth

The classic exposition of 'experimental faith' as a means of discovering truth is to be found in William James' *The Will to Believe*. James argues that: 'a rule of thinking which would absolutely prevent me from

---

[3] (New York: Bantam Books, 1984).

acknowledging certain kinds of truth, if those certain kinds of truth were really there would be an irrational rule.'[4] The rule he has in mind is that expressed in W. K. Clifford's dictum, quoted earlier: 'It is wrong always, everywhere, and for everyone to believe anything upon insufficient evidence.'[5] On the contrary, James maintains, if promising hypotheses are to be adequately tested, one must be prepared to persevere with them over a reasonable period of time. Otherwise healthy brain-children may be killed off by premature antisepsis. Moreover, there are in life certain choices which are 'lively, forced and momentous' with respect to which the option of suspending judgement is not available. Moral choices and choices of one's entire philosophy of life are among these. When what is at stake is the possibility of coming to know and love a personal God, the need for an initial commitment is even greater and more obvious, so that James' argument lends particular support to a distinctively theistic faith.

The argument gains additional support from John Stuart Mill in his plea for freedom of speech. He observes that, in general, truth is better served by having a variety of systems of belief in vigorous competition with one another than by allowing the expression only of what is currently held to be the truth. This policy favours the optimum development of the rival systems by encouraging creativity and ensuring the exposure of each of them to the most determined criticism.

If the policies of James and Mill are to succeed, two

[4] (London: Longmans, 1902), 28.
[5] Quoted by James, *ibid.*

extremes are to be avoided. One is dogmatism, understood as a state of mind which is impervious to criticism.
A system of belief dogmatically adhered to will simply
ossify, and will not undergo those modifications which
are necessary, in changing circumstances, to maintaining
its identity. The other is complete open-mindedness: the
putative system will be subject to so many fluctuations
as not to develop a coherent identity at all.

In the light of these considerations it would seem that
the tendency of people to develop persistent convictions
which are underdetermined by the evidence is not only a
widespread phenomenon, as Newman noted, but one
that is justified as a means to discovering truth. Truth is
more likely to be found if people join together in
developing a set of ideas with a considerable degree of
perseverance than if they allow their opinions to
fluctuate readily in response to changes in the evidence.

It may be objected that what this line of argument
shows is something less than is being claimed for it.
Granted that the most profitable strategy for the
discovery of truth may often involve a readiness to go
beyond the evidence, it does not require belief, let alone
conviction. All that is needed is a readiness to act *as if* the
relevant hypotheses were true rather than actually to
believe them.

In order to take the measure of this objection we need
to remind ourselves once again of the sort of situation in
which such faith is required. It is one in which the
system of thought to which one adheres is under
challenge. The cases in question are those in which,
from the standpoint of such a system, things 'look bad'.
They are recognizably situations of temptation in which

we acknowledge a duty not to give up prematurely as soon as the going gets difficult. The great pioneers of science and other disciplines were people who survived crises, sometimes prolonged, in which everything seemed to be against them.

The problems of anyone thus situated are accentuated by the fact that among the things which morally tempt one to give up will be found some considerations which owe their effectiveness as temptations to their seeming to provide good reasons why we should do so—although in fact they do not. Even in academic life, in spite of its comparative calm, people are exposed to pressures which are not wholly rational and which sometimes, to make things worse, masquerade as rational. Intellectual fashions, for example, are very powerful and so are academic reputations, and no-one who has lived through a period of unremitting pressure can have failed to be aware how linguistic conventions and even facial expressions and tones of voice are brought into play to reinforce a particular line of thought. In such circumstances, when arguments are made by such adventitious devices to seem more persuasive than they are, it is far from easy to make at all times a calm and rational assessment of the state of play. If the position you represent is to have any chance at all of making good its claims, you will have to hang on to it, suspecting that you cannot always take the considerations advanced against it at their face value, and realizing that you are often unable here and now to undertake the cool and complete assessment which is ideally required. The position is this: I want to adhere to that system of belief which, in some form or other, is most likely to turn out to be true in the long run. But how likely is it that I, situated as I am, with my known limitations and all the pressures upon me, am going to be able to make a just assessment of all the issues involved and distinguish clearly between what I have good reason to believe and what I am entertaining simply as a promising hypothesis? It may sometimes be feasible, if the outcome does not matter very much, to maintain this sort of detachment, but as a rule it is not humanly possible. Not experimental hypotheses, but only persistent convictions will succeed in surviving the trial.

It is, of course, as we have already seen, essential that the state of the evidence should be kept in review, if truth is indeed to be approached. Otherwise weaknesses will not be recognized as weaknesses and corrections will not be made where they are needed. The individual who persists in a conviction when the evidence is, as it stands, inadequate, does at least believe that it will in the end turn out to be the case, when all the evidence is gathered in, that it will, in some recognizable form, be vindicated.

These are some of the reasons why a certain persistence in people's convictions is required if the chances of achieving, or at least approximating to, the truth are to be maximized. Some of the considerations I have mentioned involve psychological rather than strictly cognitive factors, but they are not unrelated to the latter. Human beings are not uniformly rational and any policies directed to the discovery of truth must take this into account.

(b) The search for salvation

Religion, unlike metaphysics, is not concerned solely

with truth. It has to do primarily with liberation or salvation. And, in a broad enough sense of the words, this is the case also with secular world-views or philosophies of life in so far as they offer a faith to live by. Each envisages an unsatisfactory state of affairs from which the individual needs to be 'saved' or 'liberated', a means of effecting the rescue and a final situation in the attainment of which the rescue consists. As Swinburne puts it, 'there is in each case a way, a creed and a goal'.[6]

It follows from what has been said earlier that it is necessary to go on following the way for long enough to have a reasonable chance of attaining the goal. Since there are what look like other ways purporting to lead to the same or other goals, questions of truth are involved. Hence the need for the associated creed, which makes such factual claims as that:

(i) Such and such a way will lead to such and such a goal. Where the goal is a purely internal one, for instance an experience of liberation as in Buddhism, the creed can be simple and in little danger of being contradicted by scientific or historical evidence. When, as in Christianity, it is envisaged as the consummation of the entire historical process, there is an appreciable risk of a clash with scientific and historical knowledge. In such a case, belief that the way will lead to its intended goal presupposes that the world is so constituted as to make this possible.

(ii) Such and such a goal will prove ultimately

---

[6] Richard Swinburne, *Faith and Reason* (Oxford: Clarendon Press, 1981), 125 ff.

satisfying. According to most philosophies of life and all religions the goal includes the attainment of a certain state of character, if indeed it does not consist wholly in this; and the way involves the persistent attempt to develop the right sort of character (in Christian terms, sanctification). Any way will be beset by temptations of the sort we have already considered. The pilgrim will be under pressure to abandon the journey for reasons which will seem at the time convincing; that the way is getting him nowhere, that the goal is not worth the difficulties and dangers of achieving it, or is illusory or less worth striving for than some alternative. The predicament of any such pilgrim is that without perseverance no worthwhile goal can be achieved, yet he or she cannot have complete assurance of being on the right path to the right goal.

In deciding whether to persevere in a way or not, it will be relevant how valuable is the goal to which one hopes it may lead and how stringent the obligations it is believed to impose. This consideration underlies the argument which, in different forms, is developed by Pascal and Butler to the effect that the promise of a very great reward warrants a degree of perseverance commensurate with it. This is one reason why theistic belief inspires so great a measure of commitment. A personal God is both the fount of felicity and the source of obligation.

In so far as one is more likely to follow a way with determination if one believes with full conviction that it will lead to the goal and that the goal is supremely worthwhile, there is reason to reinforce the belief so as to help one to achieve the goal. Hence the pragmatic justification of Pascal's advice about masses and holy water. Moreover, in so far as a certain state of character is part of the goal, and in view of the reciprocal relationship between conviction and character, a considerable degree of commitment is unavoidable.

It will be apparent that, if this account is at all correct, there is an inevitable tension between faith and reason in that the purely pragmatic grounds for tenacity in belief are calculated to reinforce false beliefs as well as true ones. We have an interest both in deciding which are the right goals to seek and in pursuing the chosen way resolutely. The latter requirement cannot be met if we are too easily persuaded that we are on the wrong track; the former requirement cannot be met if we refuse to heed any signs that we are going astray.

I have spoken of this as an inevitable predicament, and in the conditions of human life it seems to be so. The predicament would be mitigated or even perhaps abolished altogether, if it were possible to abandon either of the imperatives which generate it—if, that is, the demands of reason were abated or the need for commitment denied. Kierkegaard and Clifford represent the extreme poles of this dichotomy. Kierkegaard seems to say that faith is meritorious precisely to the degree that it spurns the help of reason and embraces a claim that is objectively absurd. It would seem to follow that it does not ultimately matter what is the content of belief so long as it is adhered to with sufficient intensity, a conclusion which Kierkegaard does not himself draw, but which has continued to inspire a whole tradition of existentialism in philosophy and theology. It has the paradoxical consequence that the experience of faith's being tested in the fires of critical debate is one that cannot, in logic, occur.

The inadequacies of Clifford's demand that belief should at all times be strictly proportionate to the evidence currently available has been sufficiently exposed by Pascal, Butler, and James.

If then, the predicament is unavoidable, the question arises how a proper balance is to be achieved between the demands of criticism and those of commitment. The argument suggests that to pursue a way blindly towards a goal that is inadequately apprehended will not achieve the desired end; and that, on the other hand, to allow oneself to be distracted from the pursuit of the chosen way whenever there seem to be indications, which may prove to be illusory, that one is being misled, will prevent any goal at all from being reached. It was suggested earlier that there are various strategies open to the believer when confronted by contrary evidence. They all presuppose that some modification of the creed may in fact be demanded, together with variations in the way. The creed functions as a guide to one's steps and it will not do that properly if signs and warnings are systematically ignored. There must, then, be a process by which pilgrims are able to correct their maps and check their compasses as they go along, a process which calls for alert attention to the scene as well as resolute determination not to be misled by false signals or distracted by disturbing passions.

It will by now be apparent where this whole line of argument is leading. Our initial problem was how to reconcile the readiness of liberal theologians to expose their beliefs to criticism with the unconditional commitment characteristic of religious faith. Underlying this problem, as generally presented, is a contrast between secular rationality and Christian faith, the former, as represented by natural science, entirely impartial and open-minded, with confidence proportioned, in the manner of W. K. Clifford, to the evidence available at any given time; the latter firm and unwavering and impervious to criticism.

It now appears that this simple contrast will not do. The conditions of human life are such that in all matters of importance to us we have to choose between alternative schemes of thought which have varying degrees of rational support but which cannot be shown to be true beyond all dispute. In so far as we have to act in the world, choices have to be made, and in so far as our actions have to be consistent, our choices need to be consistent too, that is to say they have to be based on some more or less coherent view of the world. Our choice of such a view of the world determines not only what we do, but also to a large extent, who we are. It is not sensible or, indeed, possible, in this predicament, to be constantly changing our stance, because in that case we should not adhere to our convictions long enough to put them to the test, or to effect worthwhile changes in the world, or to develop for ourselves a consistent character. So there is need for faith (or at least for some secular analogue of it), in virtue of which we can hold to our course, whatever it is, when the going gets difficult, as from time to time it always does.

But, having said this, I must insist once again that it is no virtue to adhere to one's position no matter what the evidence against it. There is such a thing as unreasoning

prejudice and we may also be tempted to go on believing
something when we ought no longer to do so. An
obstinate policy of refusing to accept plain facts or
acknowledge good arguments can only result in failure
to revise one's opinions, so that eventually they no
longer apply to the world as it is. At the extreme it
becomes the sort of paranoia which turns the edge of all
criticism by interpreting it in terms of the dominant
delusion. Faith is adherence to genuine beliefs and not to
delusional fantasies or mechanical formulae which are
no longer responsive to the way things are. An amusing
example (at least it seems amusing in retrospect,
although it was tragic enough at the time) is provided by
Alain Peyrefitte in his book *Le Mal Francais*,[7] in which
he accuses his fellow countrymen of preferring abstract
theories to the evidence of their senses (a tendency he
blames upon Descartes). He narrates how in May 1940
the pilot of a French aircraft in the neighbourhood of
the Ardennes Forest noticed a column of German tanks
proceeding in the direction of Paris. As soon as he
landed he reported to his commanding officer who duly
relayed the information to Headquarters, who totally
refused to believe it. So the commanding officer, who
was a trained observer, went up himself as well, and this
time they both saw two columns of tanks in roughly the
same area. On returning to base the commanding officer
rang up Headquarters and insisted on speaking to the
general in person. The general listened politely and then
replied very firmly that the alleged sighting must be a
mistake, because France's entire defensive strategy was

[7] (Paris: Plan, 1976), 16–17.

predicated upon the principle that enemy tanks could not penetrate the French defensive line, of which the Ardennes Forest was part.

I said at an earlier stage, when discussing the duties of academics, that while neutrality is not demanded, impartiality and fair-mindedness are. And these involve sensitivity to criticism and, equally important, sensitivity to critics. If this is lacking, beliefs will not be developed or refined, and it is surely a failure in conviction rather than a demonstration of it, not to explore the full significance of one's beliefs or not to exploit their possibilities.

It is, perhaps, significant that I made this point in relation to academics. For it is evident that not everyone has this particular duty to quite the same extent. Many, perhaps most, believers are not accustomed to making their beliefs explicit and examining and re-examining their grounds for holding them, and their faith is no less sincere for that. (Newman's favourite example was the Irish peasant woman.) Although it is not a special obligation laid upon intellectuals, it is an obligation that applies especially to them; and any movement, whether secular or religious, requires its intellectuals to perform this function on its behalf.

It is often said, in defence of academic institutions, that their role is that of criticizing the accepted ideas of our society; and that, of course, is true, but it is only half the truth. They have a role in maintaining and developing them too. There is a need for balance in the intellectual life which I can, perhaps, best bring out by instancing the vocation of the individual teacher. A good teacher has a duty both to encourage and to criticize the pupil and the art of teaching lies in the proper balance between encouragement and criticism. It is often thought that, the more advanced the level of study, the less teaching matters, so that graduate students need no teaching at all and professors do not need to be good teachers—they need only know their subject. Not so—the good graduate student needs encouragement that his or her own ideas are worth developing and can be made to yield genuine illumination. But criticism also is essential if what is good and bad in these ideas is to be distinguished so that they can be developed in their strongest form. Premature and unsympathetic criticism can easily dry up the springs of inspiration at their source.

The individual scholar has to internalize those same principles in his or her own work. Constant self-criticism inhibits creativity and there must be periods of relatively expansive reflection when ideas are left to unroll themselves without continuous checking. I was once told by a very distinguished historian, whose name I dare not reveal, that he generally preferred to review a book before he had read it, because he found his ideas muddled by the actual text. He then read the book and altered his review when necessary which was, however, so he assured me, comparatively rarely.

In all this, in spite of their specialized function, scholars are no different from human beings in general. The discussion so far, although it has emphasized the close links between theory and practice, could easily give the impression that the problems we have considered have no direct bearing upon everyday life, whereas we encounter them inescapably in our dealings with people.

Our conception of what it is to be a human being profoundly affects the way we treat people and the way we think we ought to treat them. There is, in fact, a reciprocal relationship between our intuitive judgements about people and our immediate responses to them and the more theoretical ideas about them that we have imbibed from our culture whether we are aware of them or not. Few of us have been untouched by Freud, however unconvinced we may be by his somewhat mechanistic account of the workings of the unconscious. We are likely to have been influenced also by a whole complex of notions, going back to the Enlightenment, and beyond it to Christianity and Judaism and the concepts of Roman law and Greek philosophy. We often see better than we know, but how we see is not independent of what we have learnt. And here, right at the heart of our personal life, we are confronted once again by the tension between faith and criticism. For the conceptions that we have of human personality, based as they are upon the psychological theories of Freud and all these earlier influences, are themselves controversial, in the sense that they are subject to correction and capable of further development. We cannot regard them, abstractly considered, as being in their presently accepted form so firmly established that no alternative theories have any chance of proving right. Yet we cannot and do not, in the actual conduct of our lives, treat them merely as hypotheses to be accepted only tentatively.

The firm conviction that D. Z. Phillips noticed in the 139th Psalm can be seen equally in serious love poetry:

> How many loved your moments of glad grace,
> And loved your beauty with love false or true;
> But one man loved the pilgrim soul in you,
> And loved the sorrows of your changing face.

A whole philosophy is encapsulated in that 'pilgrim soul' and it is one that can be, and often has been, controverted. It has Platonic as well as Christian overtones. So perhaps the poet, knowing this, ought to have qualified his utterance and said: 'But one man loved what he plausibly identified as the "pilgrim soul" in you or what, according to certain defensible theories of human nature, may reasonably be regarded as a "pilgrim soul".' But the kind of love he has for her depends upon his seeing her in this way. Perhaps no-one whose intellectual formation was wholly modern or 'post-modern' could think of a person so. A. S. Byatt in her novel *Possession* says of one of her contemporary characters:

Roland had learned to see himself, theoretically, as a crossing place for a number of systems, all loosely connected. He had been trained to see his idea of his 'self' as an illusion, to be replaced by a discontinuous machinery and electrical message-network of various desires, ideological beliefs and responses, language-forms and hormones and pheromones. Mostly he liked this. He had no desire for any strenuous Romantic self-assertion.[8]

It is no accident, then, that the two contemporary characters in the book, of whom Roland is one, do not know how to fall in love. For a tale of wholehearted Romantic love the author has to go back into the

[8] (London: Chatto and Windus, 1990), 459.

nineteenth century, and the contrast between the two periods makes the fascination of the book.

Before proceeding, in the next chapter, to address directly the problem of faith and criticism where the faith intended is religious faith, let me endeavour to sum up the conclusions we have so far reached.

The chief conclusion is that human beings are so constituted that they need to develop convictions that are both stable and, so far as possible, rational—that is to say, tested against knowledge and experience. Given the comprehensiveness and complexity of the situations with which we have to deal, our convictions are such that:

(*a*) although they are, for the most part, rationally based, the total case for them is a cumulative one, which we are normally unable to articulate fully and cannot generate entirely on our own. They are shared with others and related to a common tradition.

(*b*) they contribute to making us the sort of people we are. There is, that is to say, a close reciprocal connection between convictions and character.

(*c*) for this reason they are comparatively stable. Although, in so far as they are rational they are responsive to criticism, and we acknowledge an obligation to defend them against criticism; we do not take all criticisms equally seriously and we do not reckon to abandon our convictions whenever we encounter criticisms that we cannot then and there readily rebut.

(*d*) nevertheless, the obligation to be responsive to criticism means that we cannot simply ignore criticism in the long run. To do so would convert our convictions into unreasoning prejudices and risk eventually emptying them of all significance. In order the more fully to understand them and their implications we have to be prepared to modify them or, at least, our current interpretation of them.

(*e*) this obligation to respond to criticism is not laid upon all equally. It is a duty particularly of intellectuals and is one they perform on behalf of the community generally. It would be absurd to claim that only intellectuals possess convictions just because they are, as a rule, better able to articulate them; but it would be equally absurd to deny them convictions because they can see, more clearly than most, the arguments against them.

(*f*) it is inherent in the nature of convictions that they might ultimately turn out to be mistaken and that, in that event, one ought to give them up. If I have emphasized in this chapter the need to resist temptation to abandon one's convictions prematurely rather than the obligation to give them up eventually if and when the time is ripe, this is in order to redress the balance. The impression is so often created that to change one's mind about these matters is a relatively easy thing and that a reasonable person will have no difficulty in recognizing when the moment has come to do so, whereas in fact it is, as a rule, desperately painful to revise one's convictions radically and hard to know when the crisis point has come. Meanwhile there are bound to be innumerable occasions when the individual will be tempted to abandon convictions but ought not to do so, and it is in just such situations that he or she needs the capacity to recognize the temptation for what it is and to hold out against it.

This capacity clearly has a great deal in common with religious faith. In the next chapter we must go on to consider whether religious faith is, indeed, in any respects different. If it were to turn out not to be, it is already, I think, apparent that a good deal of the criticism directed against the liberal theologian fails to hit the mark. For the kind of conviction (or 'faith' if that is the right word) that I have been describing is not, in any sense, merely tentative and provisional. It governs a person's whole life and is persistent and deeply committed.

But is it 'unconditionally committed'? That is the question to which we must now turn.

3

Faith and Criticism as Interdependent

The time has come to apply to the specific case of religious faith what we have learned about convictions in general, and then to see what else needs to be said.

The main thrust of my argument has been to the effect that the charge that to accept the possibility of criticism is to rule out commitment is palpably untrue to the way our thinking really works in matters of any importance, whether religious or not. Even in the realm of the natural sciences, where the advancement of knowledge is the central concern and where the subject matter is strictly delimited, a considerable degree of tenacity is required if new theories are to be adequately tested and properly developed. Hence, established scientific systems are not abandoned in the face of problems and puzzles that are not immediately soluble. Science advances precisely by the sustained attempt to iron out these anomalies.

In the human sciences and the humanities, emotions and habitual attitudes come increasingly into the reckoning. Here, the larger questions are normally to some extent controversial, and practitioners have no choice but to persevere in some particular approach to the subject, which they share with others, thus maintaining a tradition and subscribing to a recognizable 'school of thought'. Such academic disciplines frequently overlap with world-views or philosophies of life, which have moral as well as other practical implications. The latter offer the individual a 'faith to live by' and in living by them he or she develops a distinctive character. Convictions are not the sort of things we just happen to have and which we could shed at a moment's notice; we are the people we are largely because of the convictions which we have made our own and which in turn have shaped us. They affect the way we see the world, how we view other people and how we respond to them. In our relations with others, especially those we know and love, we have no alternative but to trust them, and that implies also trusting the convictions that we have about what people in general are like. Of course we do not, when we are trying to help someone in distress, theorize consciously about the causes and effects of suffering or the nature and degrees of moral responsibility, but we draw upon all our resources of understanding in such a situation. As Iris Murdoch says 'We act rightly "when the time comes" not out of strength of will but out of the quality of our usual attachments and with the kind of energy and discernment which we have available. And to this the whole activity of our consciousness is relevant.'[1] In so doing we commit ourselves to judgements about these matters which, when coolly considered, we can see to be open to dispute. It is not that

[1] *The Sovereignty of Good* (London: Routledge & Kegan Paul, 1970), 91–2.

they have no rational foundation—although, since our grasp of them is generally tacit or implicit, we are not generally able to display it fully—but rather that there are, and we know that there are, intelligent people who would challenge them. 'We hold these truths to be self-evident, that all men are created equal.' We all of us respond to this declaration with complete commitment. Yet Plato and Aristotle did not share it and they were not fools.

If I may be autobiographical for a moment, the most difficult decision I personally have ever had to make was at the beginning of the Second World War—and I suppose this is true of many others. I had just finished my degree in philosophy at Oxford and had to decide whether I should fight in the war or register as a conscientious objector. In my generation of students there was a distinct, if somewhat confused, strain of pacifism, and I was strongly inclined to take the latter course. My family had been deeply involved with the Sufi Movement which held that essentially the same truth was to be found in all religions. Largely because of this I had begun to study Indian philosophy as a graduate student. Some of my friends directed my attention to the *Bhagavadgita* which I was reading in Sanskrit at the time. For that noble poem begins with the very situation that was exercising us. Arjuna, the warrior, is about to fight a battle and among the opposing army are some close relatives of his. He is overcome by indecision: should he fight or not? The entire poem is a dialogue on this question between Arjuna and his charioteer, who is the god Krishna in disguise. Krishna argues that what matters supremely is not what Arjuna does, what changes he brings about in the world by his actions, but the attitude of mind in which he does whatever he does. The intention is everything; the outcome is indifferent. 'That man whose every enterprise is without desire or motive, whose work is burnt up in the fire of knowledge, the wise call learned. Having cast off attachment to the fruit of work, contented ever and on none dependent, though he engage himself in work, yet works he not at all.'[2] 'Hold equal pleasure and pain, gain and loss, victory and defeat, then gird thyself for battle: thus shalt thou not gather to thee guilt.'[3] But, since Arjuna is a member of the warrior caste, a *Kshatriya*, his duty or *dharma* is to fight.

I looked again at the *Gita* and was deeply moved, as who could fail to be, but I was not convinced. When it came to the point I found myself quite unable to believe that what happened in the world as the result of my actions was not of ultimate importance. To be sure it mattered little what I, as a single individual, did as the German tanks rolled into France, but what thousands like me did might make a crucial difference to the course of human history. At that moment I discovered myself to be profoundly occidental.

I do not suppose that even now I can render fully explicit what lay behind that conviction, but it had, I believe, something to do with the Christian pattern of Creation and Redemption and a consequent vision of the world as the theatre of irrevocable choices. The

---

[2] *Bhagavadgita*, tr. W. O. D. Hill (Oxford, 1928), 4th Reading, vv. 18–21.   [3] *Ibid.* 2nd Reading, v. 38.

point is well made by Helen Gardner in a discussion of
tragedy:

The mystical conception, fundamental in the great religions
of the East, of the soul as imprisoned in matter, and of
redemption as salvation and escape from the world of time
and the flesh, is incompatible with the sense that all our
experience in this world has value and meaning which would
seem to inspire the tragic poet ... Religions which preach
withdrawal from the world of human action, and train the
human spirit in detachment from its fellows, teaching it to
aspire towards 'the flight of the Alone to the Alone', or to the
bliss of Nirvana, put aside the tragic questions, and will not
inspire artists to find meaning in human life in its short
course in this world of illusions.[4]

Given that one's fundamental convictions operate at
this very profound level of the personality, notwithstanding that they are not universally shared and are
open to criticism by those who do not share them, it is
evident that Phillips's rewriting of the 139th Psalm as, in
his view, it ought to be recited by someone who
acknowledges these facts, although splendid entertainment, is a complete travesty of the truth.

In considering this kind of example of the way in
which our basic convictions work we have already
arrived at the case of religious faith, and the ease of the
transition strongly suggests that there is no fundamental
difference between it and the non-religious cases we
examined earlier. Nevertheless, opponents of the liberal
position might still not be satisfied. They might doubt
whether the religious faith we have arrived at by this

---

[4] *Religious Literature* (London: Faber & Faber, 1971), 95.

route can be genuine Christian faith as they understand
it.

Up to this point, I have in effect been operating with
what sociologists call a 'functional' approach to the
definition of religious faith and stressing analogies
between religious and other systems of belief which
afford meaning to human life in both personal and
public spheres. That sociologists are able, for certain
purposes, to define religion in this way lends support to
my use of these analogies. I have been suggesting that
the tension between faith and criticism which is
experienced by religious believers also affects the adherents of non-religious philosophies of life. It seems to
follow that religious faith just is a special case of the sort
of adherence that human beings give to any body of
convictions which plays this central role in their lives.

But this may be denied both by unbelievers and by
believers, especially more conservative ones. They may
argue that Christian faith demands an altogether greater
degree of commitment to a particular historical tradition
than is required by these secular analogies. They may
grant that both in the past and in the present there are
plenty of examples of movements of thought, with a
greater or lesser degree of organization, which to some
extent define themselves by reference to certain historical
exemplars. To be a Stoic or an Epicurean or a
Peripatetic in the ancient world was to commit yourself
to an established philosophical tradition, and, a generation or so back, classicists like Sir Richard Livingstone
sought to distil from the study of the Greek and Roman
classics a philosophy of life suitable to our time.
Marxism and feminism, to name only two modern

movements, have their own canonical texts, acceptance of which tends to define these movements. It is true that there are continuing disputes as to which of the texts are the most authoritative and how the various ones are to be interpreted, but this serves to strengthen rather than weaken the religious analogy.

Nevertheless, they may insist that Christian faith cannot be a purely individual matter but involves sharing the creed of the Christian Church; and that the Church itself accepts the authority of the Scriptures and of the Christian tradition more definitely and more formally than is the case with these secular counterparts.

There are contemporary theologians of a liberal temper who would deny this altogether and would maintain that theology is an entirely open-ended enquiry. There is, as they see it, no difference between the Christian theologian's attitude to the Bible and the Christian tradition and that of a philosophical scholar to, say, Plato or Aristotle. In each case the aim is to understand what writers of the past meant, in the light of all the evidence available, and to appropriate whatever is found to be of permanent value. A contemporary philosopher may be a Platonist or an Aristotelian or a Kantian, convinced that the root of the matter is to be found in these thinkers and prepared to defend that conviction. Theologians, on this view of the matter, approach the Bible in a precisely similar way. Scripture is authoritative only to the extent that worthwhile insights are to be found in it, which survive subsequent testing.

Such a stance, although possible for a theologian, is not characteristic, but its prevalence does throw into

relief features of Christian faith, as traditionally understood, which are thought to impose particular strains
upon the believer, strains which are avoided altogether
or at least are felt less severely, by the secular thinker.
(Hence the familiar term 'freethinker' for an atheist or
agnostic.) The believer is committed to the faith of the
Church, which in turn is committed to the historic faith
of Christians. Each element in this double commitment
is felt to impede the free flow of enquiry which is a
necessary condition of rational criticism. Hence the
arguments I adduced in my last chapter in favour of
adherence to a continuous tradition as a means of
approaching truth are not available to Christian faith.
The individual believer surrenders his rights of criticism
to the Church and the Church systematically prejudges
all issues by acceptance of an authority which cannot be
questioned.

Conservative objectors accept this critique willingly
and acknowledge freely that it does decisively weaken
the analogies we have been developing. For unlike the
sort of secular conviction we have been considering,
Christian faith is not a human achievement but a gift
from God. And this in two senses: what is believed is not
some system of ideas which men have constructed or
discovered but a set of revealed truths; and the
acceptance of it both corporately in the Church and
privately in the individual Christian is the product not of
a human decision but of a God-given grace. Moreover,
faith establishes a real relationship with God: it is not a
matter simply of forming and accepting a defensible
conception of God but of coming to know and love him.
This objection is to be found trenchantly expressed in

the writings of Karl Barth. Barth insists on the need to subordinate all philosophical and empirical criticism to the story of God's action in Christ as Creator, Reconciler, and Redeemer.

In an attempt to meet this objection which has considerable weight I propose now to pause and start afresh, so to speak, from the other end. Let us take the central commandment of the Judaeo-Christian tradition: 'Thou shalt love the Lord thy God with all thy heart and with all thy soul and with all thy mind and with all thy strength and thy neighbour as thyself.' What does this require of us in respect of belief?

It means at the very least that we must be alert to all signs that God is speaking to us and be loyal in thought and deed to what he tells us. Let us assume, what is true of most of us, that we have been brought up as Christians or, at any rate, within the ambit of Christianity. (And we have to remember that something similar is true of everyone. No matter what an individual's present convictions and conceptions, he or she has not entirely invented them but derives them in large part from an existing tradition or traditions.) As Christians, then, we have been taught to hear God speaking to us in the Bible and in the tradition of the Church. Simply to repeat what is said in the Bible without any attempt to understand it will scarcely be worthy to be called listening to it;

(*a*) it is to give the word of God less respect than we would give to any human teacher and to ignore the instruction of scripture itself to 'mark, learn, and inwardly digest'.

(*b*) the Bible says different things in different places

and, as becomes quickly evident, at different times. We are compelled, therefore, to discriminate, if we are truly to hear the word of God. There must be a process of subordinating some parts of the Bible to others. (*c*) we must expect to grow in understanding. This is certainly true of us as individuals. We all have to develop beyond the faith that satisfied us as children; and we ought surely to expect that God's truth will transcend our understanding at any particular time and indeed prove inexhaustible. Though we may progress in the understanding of it, we shall never be in a position to claim that we comprehend it fully. 'For now we see through a glass darkly.' If this is true of individuals, it must no less be true of the Church as an institution. If the Holy Spirit is to lead us into all truth, it follows that we do not have the full truth now.

What has been said so far is, perhaps, not contentious. It is, of course, over-simple, but in broad outline most Christians would accept it. The difficulties arise when we consider what is involved in discrimination and understanding.

Discrimination implies that we possess criteria by which we are able to determine what is genuine and what is not, what is authoritative and what is not. This is, in a broad sense of the word, an exercise of reason. Understanding implies a capacity on our part to recognize what makes sense and what does not and to conclude that some interpretations make better sense than others. It is a principle of reason that truth is one, that truths cannot contradict one another, so that in interpreting what presents itself as the word of God we are bound to prefer that interpretation which coheres best with the rest of our knowledge. The principle is vigorously expounded by John Locke in a splendid piece of seventeenth-century prose:

Faith can never convince us of anything that contradicts our knowledge. Because, though faith be founded on the testimony of God (who cannot lie) revealing any proposition to us; yet we cannot have an assurance of the truth of its being a divine revelation greater than our knowledge; since the whole strength of the certainty depends upon our knowledge that God revealed it; which in this case, where the proposition supposed revealed contradicts our knowledge and reason, will always have this objection hanging to it, *viz*, that we cannot tell how to know that to come from God, the bountiful Author of our being, which, if received for true, must overturn all the principles and foundations of knowledge he has given us; render all our faculties useless; wholly destroy the most excellent part of his workmanship, our understanding; and put a man in a condition wherein he will have less light, less conduct than the beast that perisheth.[5]

It is to be noted that Locke places his main emphasis upon the incoherence that would be involved in God's overturning 'the principles and foundations of knowledge he has given us'. He differs from Barth, that is to say, and assumes, as did Aquinas, that human reason has, by divine gift, a genuine, although derived, authority.

Let us consider the way in which we respond to a human teacher. Simply to repeat what the teacher says is no indication of understanding it. We must be able to 'put it into our own words', to answer questions about

[5] *Essay*, Book IV, ch. XVIII, 5.

it, to apply it to situations which the teacher did not originally envisage, and so on. As Wittgenstein used to put it, we need to be able 'to go on from there'. Three students may listen to a lecture and be asked to expound the lecturer's views. One copies down the lecture verbatim and returns it as his essay; another, not having paid very careful attention, composes a lively essay of her own on the subject and ascribes her own views to the lecturer; a third is inspired by the lecture to develop its theme and apply it to fresh examples in such a way that the teacher says, 'I might have written it myself'.

Those of us who are teachers will have enjoyed the experience just occasionally of having a pupil who understood us so well as to enter into the spirit of our thinking and think our own thoughts for us in different language from our own and in fresh contexts. Of course, in so doing, the pupil thinks his or her own thoughts, but the outcome of this creative endeavour is an accurate and sympathetic account of our thoughts. The point has been well made by, interestingly enough, Bultmann:

The demand that the interpreter must silence his subjectivity and extinguish his individuality in order to attain an objective knowledge is, therefore, the most absurd that can be imagined. It is sensible and right only in so far as we mean by it that the interpreter must silence his personal wishes with regard to the outcome of the interpretation. . . . Otherwise the demand ultimately misjudges the nature of real comprehension. For the latter presupposes the utmost liveliness of the comprehending subject, and the richest possible unfolding of his individuality.[6]

[6] *Essays Philosophical and Theological*, tr. James C. G. Greig (London: SCM Press, 1955), 255–6.

But, the critic of liberalism will complain, does not the willingness to take account of modern knowledge imply that, whenever modern knowledge conflicts with received doctrine, it is always the latter that must give way? Locke, indeed, has been interpreted in this sense. Once again the practice of some liberal theologians does lend colour to this charge. It is all too easy to loosen the hold of tradition only in turn to become enslaved to fashion. The problem is, of course, intensified when the 'modern thought' whose authority is invoked against the tradition is not straightforwardly scientific or scholarly but, rather, ideological.

But what we have said earlier about the controversial nature of most academic disciplines, not excluding the human sciences, means that what passes for 'modern knowledge' has credentials of varying strength. Where a scientific theory has the strongest possible warrant so that no reputable scientist would think of disputing it, then it is indeed the case that theologians must accept it. The broad outlines of the Darwinian theory of natural selection are a case in point (as many of the leading theologians of the nineteenth century recognized, including Newman). But where scientific findings are in dispute, it does not automatically follow that theologians are bound to adopt the majority view. This applies not only to theologians but to metaphysicians generally. For instance, contemporary physiologists tend to adopt it as a methodological principle that all mental events can be identified with changes in the brain, and many of them would for that reason accept some form of scientific determinism as a central element in their total philosophy of life. But Christian theologians and other philosophers who stress human freedom and responsibility are not bound to accept this view, and generally do not. Liberal theologians from Schleiermacher onwards have tended to accept a cautious policy of strategic retreat in face of the onward march of science. Since any territory which theology might want to hold was liable in the course of time to be invaded by science it was better, they thought, to evacuate in advance any territory which science might conceivably at a later stage lay claim to. And this territory might add up to the entire sphere of natural and human activity. Hence, God's action in the world must either be denied altogether or interpreted solely in terms of human response to the transcendent reality of God. Thus interpreted, central Christian doctrines such as the Incarnation and the Resurrection cease to imply, in any straightforward sense, the action of God in the world.

The process can be seen clearly in relation to the Resurrection. A common argument used by some liberals runs as follows: Scientific history cannot allow for the occurrence of such an event as the resurrection of Christ as traditionally understood. (I should, perhaps, add that I am not at all assuming that it is an entirely straightforward matter to interpret the tradition.) History, as a scientific discipline, cannot take account of the operation of divine causes. Hence, the evidence of the Gospels and Epistles, together with the history of the early Church, cannot give any support to the theological doctrine of the Resurrection. This doctrine has, therefore, either to be accepted entirely on faith, or to be demythologized, i.e. interpreted as the expresion of a radical change of attitude on the part of the apostles to the event of Christ's death, and not as affirming his continuing life.

However, to argue in this way is to ignore entirely the crucial difference that is made to our evaluation of the historical evidence by belief in the creative power of God. 'Scientific history', for good reason, does not take this into account, but this methodological restriction on the part of historians does not permit them to claim, on the basis of the evidence, that the Resurrection did not happen. At most they can say that, given entirely naturalistic assumptions, some other explanation is to be preferred, or failing that, that it is impossible to settle the question. (This is, in fact, a good illustration of Newman's insistence that, when interpreting evidence of any kind, a great deal depends upon one's antecedent assumptions.) Theologians, however, do not operate with entirely naturalistic assumptions. They believe and hold themselves warranted in believing that there is a God who created the world and sustains it and is able and willing to act within it for its redemption. Given this antecedent assumption, which they have independent reasons for accepting, they both can and should take the evidence as showing that God raised Jesus from the dead. The historical evidence, and with it all that goes to make up the critical scholars' apparatus, has its own integrity and cannot be made to support equally any thesis whatever. But when it comes to choosing between overall interpretations it becomes a matter of judgement how much final weight to give to the various elements in it. It simply will not do to leave it to the historians to decide what actually happened and, when they have done it, to require theologians to accept their decision as final; as determining definitively the basic historical foundations on which they have to build. I can illustrate this by a not entirely serious argument I had when an undergraduate with my tutor in ancient history. The early period of Greek history is rather short on hard evidence and there was a particular battle whose date was in question. The sole piece of evidence was that it was predicted by the Delphic oracle. The date of the oracle was known as, shall we say, 600 BC. Historians seemed to be agreed in taking this date as a *terminus ante quem* for the date of the battle, i.e. the battle must have happened before this. Why? Because, in this instance, the oracle's prediction had come true, and the oracle could only have got it right if it already knew the result. I argued in my essay that this was patently unreasonable. The oracle was a *prediction*, and the proper thing to do was to take the known date of its utterance as a *terminus post quem* for the battle, i.e. it must have happened some time after 600 BC. What right, I demanded, have historians to assume that the Delphic oracle could not predict future events? Only an unargued conviction that precognition was impossible. But (a) there was some experimental evidence for precognition, (b) the Delphic oracle would not have got a reputation for predicting the future, if it never in fact succeeded in doing so. My tutor was scandalized and we spent the rest of the tutorial arguing about precognition. I was not, as I say, wholly serious, but the principle is a valid one. It can make a difference to one's evaluation of historical evidence whether one believes in precognition or not. And this question is an extra-historical one which has to be decided on its scientific or philosophical merits.

Thus, the two considerations mentioned earlier are related: that Christian faith is not a merely human achievement and that it involves a relationship of love and trust in God. They do indeed show that our previous account is incomplete, but this admission does not impair its adequacy so far as it goes unless it is assumed that to think of faith as a divine gift is to deprive it altogether of its character as an active human response, as Barth comes close to doing. The analogy with our faith in persons holds here too. In that case as well, the purely functional approach requires to be complemented by a substantial account of what the world of things and persons is actually like, to which the individual responds by adopting and developing a scheme of beliefs and values which give meaning to life; and it makes a decisive difference whether, for example, it is a world containing Yeats' 'pilgrim souls' or A. S. Byatt's 'crossing places of loosely connected electrical systems'. It makes a difference because a faith which is bound up with trust in persons is more than the purely individual or social construction which it might otherwise be. I can learn to trust 'pilgrim souls' and come to love them, and through this experience confirm increasingly my convictions about the nature and purpose of human life. The human analogy can throw light on divine revelation too. If I encounter someone whose character and intellect I immediately recognize to be superior to my own, I shall find that he raises questions I could not have anticipated and offers answers beyond my capacity to think up myself or even fully to understand. In so doing, he enlarges my conception of what it is to be a human being and enables me to trust him as I have never before trusted anyone. It would not be inappropriate (though, perhaps, rather bathetic) to say of such a person 'he gave me faith in human nature' or 'he enhanced my faith in human nature'. From that moment on I am myself a different person. All this I have received from him and could not otherwise have come by, so far as I can tell. I certainly could not have achieved it by any amount of independent theorizing. Yet, as Bultmann notices, in grasping it and incorporating it into my own antecedent system of belief, testing it in my own experience and so on, I am exerting my own capacities to the full.

And the testing is genuine testing, which might in principle result in a decision that what had initially impressed me as a revelation of unsuspected truth was not what it had seemed to be. But before reaching any such conclusion I should have exploited all the resources available to me of intellect and imagination to ensure, so far as possible, that I had interpreted the revelation rightly.

When this comparison is applied to the case of divine revelation, it is evident, I think, that the conservative's emphasis on the primacy of divine revelation and the distinctive character of faith in it does not detract from the liberal's insistence upon the need for criticism. Rather, the two are interdependent. Criticism, to have any point, requires a strong tradition whose claims to truth are seriously advanced and will not readily be surrendered. Faith rquires that the tradition which is being upheld should be tested in the fires of criticism.

I wish to claim then that, if we start as conservatives would wish with the Christian revelation itself and what we are committed to by accepting it, there is no bar to the full exertion of our intellectual energies. It is only by exposure to criticism that the full implications of our faith can be increasingly understood, and it belongs to that faith to trust that it can withstand criticism and be illuminated by it.

I do not know of any more impressive statement of what such whole-hearted commitment involves, or one which expresses the logic of it more clearly, than Shakespeare's sonnet, 'Let me not to the marriage of true minds'—and it needs the whole sonnet to make the point:

> Let me not to the marriage of true minds
> Admit impediments. Love is not love
> Which alters when it alteration finds
> Or bends with the remover to remove;
> Oh no! it is an ever-fixed mark
> That looks on tempests and is never shaken;
> It is the star to every wandering bark,
> Whose worth's unknown, although his height be
>   taken.
> Love's not Time's fool, though rosy lips and cheeks
> Within his bending sickle's compass come;
> Love alters not with his brief hours and weeks,
> But bears it out even to the edge of doom.
> If this be error and upon me prov'd,
> I never writ nor no man ever loved.

The concluding couplet identifies the poet wholly with what he has said in the sonnet. He vouches for it with the whole of his vocation as a poet and his experience as a man. Yet, surely, the 'If this be error and upon me proved' is not purely rhetorical. It just could be error, but he stakes his entire being on its truth.

Shakespeare's faith in love (which, of course, has strong Christian overtones—one could exchange 'God' for 'love' without a change of meaning) has the same whole-hearted commitment that we saw in the writer of the 139th Psalm; and this even though Shakespeare admits it as a theoretical possibility that he might be wrong.

But, the question may be pressed, does the existence of that theoretical possibility entail that our faith, although whole-hearted, cannot be unconditional?

Faith is a word with a number of related meanings, and when this question is raised, I think that two of them have become confused. I have been talking throughout these chapters about faith in the sense of 'believing that'. To have faith in God, in that sense, is to believe that there is a God, that he created us and loves us, and so on. But there is another sense of 'faith' in which it means 'trusting reliance upon God', and it is in that sense that faith is indeed unconditional. As Christians, we are bound to maintain our trust in God's goodness and mercy no matter what dangers and difficulties confront us. Our obedience is absolute. But faith, so understood, is inextricably bound up with the whole system of Christian belief; and the fact that, within that system, faith is rightly seen as unconditional does not imply that faith in the other sense, faith in the system itself, i.e. belief that there is a God, etc., must also be unconditional. As Austin Farrer once put it, 'God cannot be trusted to exist'.

If the point seems difficult, let me illustrate it with a

sort of parable. Let us imagine a backwoodsman living in a remote part of Quebec, who believes himself to owe unconditional obedience to the King of France. He does not realize that there has not been a King of France for over a century. One day he comes into town and learns for the first time that there is no King of France and there has not been one during his lifetime. His unconditional obedience to the King of France presupposes that there is a King of France and is not to be construed as entailing an unconditional duty to go on believing that there is a King of France in the face of clear evidence to the contrary. If, in fact, there is no King of France, his obligation to obey the King of France simply fails of application.

Nevertheless, the unconditional nature of our trust in God, of our faith in him in that sense, does have a bearing on the nature of our belief in him, in the sense of 'belief that . . .', and our willingness to expose it to criticism. For it assumes that all truth is God's truth and that, if we are honest in our search for truth and at the same time loyal to the signs we have been given, we shall not ultimately be misled. We shall find the signs God has given us to be truthful, and that the truth, as we explore it, will increasingly illustrate and illuminate those signs. Those of us who are, in the sense I have given the word, liberals in theology are, I think, entitled to ask which attitude shows the greater trust in God, that which refuses to submit our traditional formulations of belief to criticism, or that which is confident that, if we put them to the test of reason and experience, we shall be led in the end to a fuller understanding of them and a firmer conviction of their truth.

4

Faith and Reason: A Problem in Navigation

I have by now sufficiently indicated the solution I wish to propose to the problem of faith and criticism as I outlined it in the first Chapter. It relies upon the claim that the dilemma in which Christian faith is said to be involved between the need for whole-hearted conviction and the requirements of rational criticism is not unique, but applies to any reflective philosophy of life. Instead of the sharp dichotomy between science and religious faith which is said to generate the dilemma, what we actually find is a continuum in which, in differing degrees, elements of faith and criticism are found at each stage.

But anyone familiar with contemporary theology will have noticed that, in developing my arguments, I have made certain assumptions which are by no means universally accepted. In particular I have taken it for granted that Christian theology has an explanatory role. I have indeed been at pains to insist that Christian faith is not merely a matter of assenting to a metaphysical theory, but I have been discussing the question of what is the proper response of Christian faith to rational criticism and this implies that it makes claims which are, in principle, open to criticism. Thus, although faith seeks salvation as well as, and more importantly than, explanation, it can achieve that goal only if its account of what the world is like and how it came to be like that is defensible. No amount of insistence upon the practical rather than the theoretical aspects of faith can alter that. The attempt that is often made to disjoin faith entirely from reason leaves the purely practical choices that are then left to us to be made in a sort of conceptual void in which no guidance can be given as to what goals are to be pursued and how or why. The serious options that actually confront us are deeply involved with subtle and complex visions of the world. Does our salvation lie in release from pain and suffering and from the bonds of a selfhood which is ultimately illusory or in release from sin through repentance and forgiveness and reconciliation with God in Christ? Or is it, perhaps, conceivable that, as John Hick would persuade us, despite differences of an apparently fundamental kind, these alternatives could eventually be found to coincide? Or is some entirely secular position to be preferred? As I found in my wrestlings with the *Bhagavadgita*, these are profound intellectual issues from which serious questions of moral and religious practice cannot be divorced.

The reluctance of many modern theologians, nevertheless, to regard them as intellectual issues which are open to rational debate, stems from the Enlightenment and in particular from the doctrines of Hume and Kant. What Hume and Kant did was to restrict drastically the scope of human reason. These restrictions operated in three ways especially:

(*a*) The traditional proofs of the existence of God

were ruled out as illegitimate because they attempted to argue from features of the world which are within our experience to the existence of a transcendent creator who is beyond our experience. Causal reasoning of the sort relied upon in the proofs could, it was maintained, operate only within the domain of human experience.

(b) This critique of metaphysical reasoning was reinforced by an equally restrictive account of what could, in principle, be understood—whether you tried to prove it or not. Our concepts are formed in response to experience of this mundane world and are unsuited to be descriptive of any other.

(c) Even if, *per impossibile*, one could conceive of a transcendent being and find good grounds for inferring his existence, there could be no warrant for claiming to discern his activity in the natural world or in the course of human history. Purely natural explanations or explanations in terms of 'scientific' history were always to be preferred.

Hume's critique, and Kant's modification of it, depended upon an identification of rational explanation as such with scientific explanation, together with a particular analysis of scientific explanation itself as the establishing of correlations between observables. Its effect was to cut the ground from beneath traditional theism and to require theologians to base their faith upon something other than rational argument. It was necessary, as Kant put it, to deny reason to make room for faith.

This they were for the most part very willing to do, the more so as the defenders of rational theology ever since Locke and the rise of natural science had tended to be aridly intellectual and out of touch with the experienced life of faith. Even Joseph Butler, who of all Christian apologists of the period was least open to this criticism, had little understanding of, or sympathy with, 'enthusiasm'; and the deists had been content to abandon the claims of revealed religion altogether. Such manifestations of rational theology could only help to intensify the romantic reaction against the claims of reason in any form. It was far better to rely instead on the sense of absolute dependence to which Schleiermacher was to appeal. In this way, not rational inference to God but a direct personal relationship with him was invoked, something so real and so immediate that adventitious intellectual supports were felt to be superfluous. Religion so understood was no longer in competition with science, which was acknowledged as the only genuine source of explanation. Hence, for Schleiermacher 'religion . . . resigns all claims on anything that belongs either to science or to morality'.[1]

Both deism and the romantic theology of Schleiermacher represent a movement in the direction of what Phillips calls 'Religion without Explanation',[2] but some minimal attempt at explanation remains. Even Schleiermacher does argue from the world to God, albeit in an informal and somewhat inchoate way. Both he and the deists can be seen as responding to Hume by jettisoning all dogmatic claims which implied God's action in the world.

[1] R. Schleiermacher, *On Religion* (New York: Harper & Row, 1958), 35.
[2] The title of his book *Religion without Explanation* (Oxford: Basil Blackwell, 1976).

However, an alternative, more radical, move was also possible. If every attempt to justify the claims of Christianity was abandoned, then the strictures of Hume and Kant could be evaded altogether without any sacrifice of the content of dogmatic claims. Such was Kierkegaard's strategy.

Or so it might seem. Kierkegaard himself may well have believed in the objective truth of Christian claims, however paradoxical these claims might be when judged by what the world regards as 'reason'; but, he insists, it requires to be appropriated by a faith whose passionate inwardness is in inverse proportion to the probability of what is asserted. It is not surprising, then, that the influence he exerted upon later thinkers was in the direction of radical subjectivity. Bultmann, for example, assumes that modern man is committed to a scientific account of the universe as a 'closed weft of cause and effect'. If as 'modern men' we are indeed committed to a scientific world-view in the sense that scientific knowledge exhausts what can be known and scientific method exhausts the ways in which we can apprehend reality, then there is no room for such Christian conceptions as those of Creation, Revelation, Redemption or Eternal Life unless they are drastically reinterpreted. Bultmann is prepared so to reinterpret them and to maintain that what look like factual assertions about supernatural realities are properly to be understood as expressions of human attitudes or profound truths about the human condition. So Bultmann can say about his 'radical attempt to demythologize the New Testament' that it: 'destroys every longing for security . . . The man who desires to believe in God must know that he has nothing at his own disposal on which to build his faith, that he is, so to speak, in a vacuum.'[3]

My account of this development corresponds in all essentials to that of Jeffrey Stout in his impressive study, *The Flight from Authority*. As he puts it:

The dialectical progression that leads from Kant and Schleiermacher to Hegel, through Hegel's followers to Marx and Kierkegaard, and finally into Barth, Bultmann and Tillich, takes Hume's accomplishment for granted and asks simply what remains possible after Hume. Post Humean theology is essentially belated; it was fathered in circumstances it would rather disown—under the rude charge of illegitimacy. Its central decision has always been whether to bear illegitimacy as a cross, the scandal of faith, or to explain the stigma away with special pleading. Either way the question is *how* not whether to make a virtue of post-Humean necessity. The attempt to refute Hume on his own terms, to revive natural theology head on, had retreated into obscure corners of the academy by the end of the Victorian period.[4]

And there Stout seems prepared to leave it and with him goes the dominant trend in modern theology, which has for the most part been entirely happy to abandon any attempt to establish religious claims by rational argument, in return for freedom to explore without hindrance the intuitive and existential reaches of human personality. The more restricted the domain of reason, the more important the area of the non-rational becomes.

We may picture the modern theologian's predicament as that of navigating a river. The pilot is endeavouring

[3] *Jesus Christ and Mythology* (New York: Scribner, 1958), 84.
[4] (Notre Dame: 1981), 128–9.

to steer his vessel successfully down to the open sea while keeping his cargo of traditional Christian doctrine so far as possible intact; at the same time avoiding the shoals which infest the channel. Shall he make for the right, rationalist, bank of the stream and adopt an apologetic which draws freely on metaphysical arguments and historical evidence; or shall he make for the left, fideist bank and put his trust entirely in faith and subjective commitment?

The chief navigational hazards are two notorious shoals, known individually as Hume and Kant and collectively as 'The Enlightenment', which lie over to the right, rationalist side of the river. The conventional wisdom is that the pilot has three options only open to him. One is to keep well over to the fideist side and sail straight past Hume and Kant. So long as no arguments are adduced in support of what he believes, or claims to know, the theologian need not be worried by their threat that any such arguments would be illegitimate. Another is to lighten the vessel by jettisoning much of its traditional cargo. Stripped of such metaphysical baggage as the concept of a transcendent God who created the world and acts in history to redeem it, the craft, thus lightened, can sail over the threatening shoals. The third option is to conclude that no craft whose cargo is worth the labour of navigating the channel has any hope of surmounting the hazards successfully. The river is simply unnavigable by theistic vessels.

What I have been assuming in this book is that there is a fourth option. It involves surveying the shoals to see if they are any longer the danger to navigation they were once thought to be. As soon as we begin this investigation

the first discovery we make is that a strict application of
the Humean test would rule out the greater part of
modern physics and cosmology, for they rely upon a
type of explanation which goes well beyond anything
that Hume would allow. Science, as Hume conceives it,
consists in the discovery of correlations between
observed phenomena, and Kant follows him in this.
They differ only as to the logical status of these
correlations. But this account is adequate, at best, to
what has been called the 'natural history stage' of
science. As one recent philosopher of science puts it:
'The discovery of correlations between observables, far
from being the end of science, is but its beginning.
Science begins when, having noted correlations, we seek
an explanation of why they obtain ... The most
profound change in science has been the development of
theories introducing ever more theoretical items and
properties for explanatory purposes.'[5]

The process had, of course, already begun before
Hume's time with the development of the atomic theory,
and is most clearly exhibited in the proliferation of sub-
microscopic particles in order to explain an ever-
increasing range of phenomena.

Not only is it an essential feature of these explanations
that, in contravention of Hume's principles, they appeal
to unobservable causes, but they also violate Hume's
requirements in another way by introducing terms that
are not straightforwardly definable by reference to our
everyday experience. Characteristic of the development

  [5] W. H. Newton-Smith, *The Rationality of Science* (London: Routledge
& Kegan Paul, 1981), 211.

of such explanatory theories is the use of 'models' whose properties do not merely represent those we usually encounter in our everyday experience, and indeed are often highly paradoxical. 'Waves' are not just like waves in the sea; 'particles' are not just like particles of dust; and their coincidence in light is paradoxical, yet they have an explanatory function and are able to suggest directions for further enquiry. They could not, that is to say, be replaced by formulae that were totally un-metaphorical.

The question whether and to what extent comparison can usefully be made between the use of models in science and religion is not for the moment at issue, although much interesting work has been done on it. The present point is a negative one only; it is that their use in scientific explanation suffices to refute the highly restrictive account of the scope and character of rationality which derives from Hume, and which has often persuaded theologians to give up any serious attempt to maintain and develop a theistic metaphysic.

It is true that the philosophy of science is (like all branches of philosophy) a controversial subject, and there are philosophers who, in deference to broadly empiricist principles, seek to interpret these developments in science in a purely instrumental or relativist way. They deny that science has or seeks any genuinely explanatory role or that it has any tendency even to approximate to the truth about the way things are. In my experience, practising scientists react to these de-mythologizers with the same mixture of irritation and impatience as do ordinary believers in the face of their theological counterparts.

Hume's attempts to limit the scope of reason are open to a further objection. Not only do they fail to do justice to the procedures of science, which they were designed to explicate, but they cannot account for the philosophical reasoning of which they are themselves examples. A comprehensive philosophical theory, such as Hume's, sets out a case which is open to the threat of counter-examples, which unless satisfactorily dealt with, remain as objections to it. It is in contention with rival theories which offer a different and, arguably, better interpretation of the matters under review. Deductive and inductive reasoning, as Hume understands them, cannot settle these issues.

The present discussion affords a case in point. If all reasoning, including philosophical reasoning, is deductive or inductive in form, the only way to establish this thesis is to examine prima-facie instances of genuine reasoning and see if they are indeed of the required forms. On the face of it, historical reasoning—to take the most obvious example—is not: is it, therefore, a counter-example which is fatal to the thesis? Inductive reasoning alone cannot answer this question which involves philosophical enquiry of a different kind.

This does not, of course, settle the issue, which remains controversial. It can, however, be asserted with reasonable confidence that the Humean critique of religious claims no longer possesses the unchallenged intellectual authority which theologians in the modern period have tended to give it. Hence Schleiermacher's strategy of surrendering to science all concern with explanation and reserving to religion some quite distinct domain no longer has the obviousness that was once claimed for it. It becomes instead increasingly plausible to hold that science and religion are, with respect to rationality, in the same boat. Either they can both surmount the shoals or neither of them can. That there are important differences between religion and science I am taking entirely for granted. All I wish to maintain is that there is not that sharp dichotomy between scientific explanation and other kinds of explanation which led so many nineteenth-century thinkers to dismiss rational theology as beyond redemption. There is, instead, a continuum of rational disciplines from physics and chemistry through the biological and social sciences to the humanities and metaphysics. Each discipline allows, in appropriate ways, of 'inference to the best explanation'. At the scientific end of the spectrum there are certain fairly precise patterns of argument possible (largely because of restrictions upon their scope) which it is tempting to equate with rationality as such. But at each stage in the continuum, not excluding the first, there is discernible a broader type of rationality in which rival explanations are canvassed and defensible choices made between them. The degree of analogy between each stage and the next, and the evident continuity between them, make it highly implausible to suggest that at some point in the sequence we encounter a decisive break such that, up to that point we have been making reasonable judgements; beyond it only existential decisions—or something of the sort.

As we saw in the first Chapter, the idea that there is such a decisive break is assisted by the tendency to make a straight comparison between natural science on the one hand and theology on the other, while overlooking entirely the intermediate disciplines. But this contrast itself is commonly attended by two misconceptions whose popular influence it would be hard to exaggerate:

(*a*) Science deals with literal truth. It tells us the way things are. Religion deals with myth and metaphor. Like poetry, it is a matter of how one feels—it has nothing to do with truth.

(*b*) Scientific questions admit of a precise decision-procedure; religious questions do not.

With respect to the first misconception, mention has already been made of the role of models and metaphors in science. Whatever view one takes about the claims of realism in the philosophy of science, there is no warrant whatever for the popular view that science and science alone provides us with a literal description of the way things are. The most that can reasonably be asserted is that, as a particular science advances and the models employed in it are modified and qualified, the resulting apparatus of theory can be judged to approximate ever more closely to the reality which is being explored.

The other side of the antithesis—that religion deals in myth and metaphor—may be freely conceded. What is open to question, however, is the interpretation that is commonly put upon this fact, viz. that, unlike scientific models, the metaphorical language of religion has a purely expressive function and is not designed to convey truth. To some extent, as we have seen, this is simply a consequence of the general tendency in our culture since the Enlightenment to assimilate all serious non-scientific uses of language to poetry, and to deny to poetry itself any concern with truth. To some extent it reflects, in addition to this, a worry about the capacity of human

language to capture the transcendent. Both were effectively criticized many years ago by Austin Farrer. In an
article entitled 'On Poetic Truth' he argued that poetry
is essentially descriptive (I think that is too strong—I
should say that it has a genuinely descriptive role) and
that what it describes is unique:

But what can we say about that which is truly unique? We may
say that it is itself, but that's not very illuminating. One can get a
certain pleasure out of it, as lovers from the repetition of the
beloved person's name or even from an excessive use of the
second person pronoun. But if we want to get beyond
'Daphne, Daphne, Daphne' or 'you, you, you', and say
something *about* the shepherdess, there really seems nothing
left but comparison, metaphor, and simile.

So he continues:

The poet is a man who has a gift for grasping fresh and
profound resemblances, and that is why he works with
metaphor and why his metaphors illuminate the nature of
things. This gift can work only by inspiration.[6]

The uniqueness and transcendence of God, he goes on to
argue, is then a reason why the language of metaphor is
most apt for talking of him. But, he insists, the
stretching of ordinary language which this involves is
not a linguistic device peculiar to our talk of God; it is a
familiar feature of everyday speech in so far as it
approximates to poetry, as it frequently does.

The failure of philosophical critics of religious
language to recognize this—and of very many theologians too—is a legacy from the empiricist tradition of

[6] In Charles C. Conti (ed.), *Reflective Faith* (London: SPCK, 1972), 31.

Hobbes, Locke, and Hume, as has been carefully documented by Janet Soskice in her fascinating study, *Metaphor and Religious Language.*

Thus, to take one of the central assertions of the Christian tradition, 'God is our Father': We can discern in it elements of positive analogy—loving concern, readiness to hear our cry, trustworthiness; and of negative analogy—physical generation, mortality, gender. Those we do not want to assert of God. The model can be developed further as by Soskice herself:

The implications of this model were drawn out in the Gospels and Epistles, and continue to be drawn out: if God is our Father, he will hear us when we cry to him; if God is our Father, then as children and heirs we come to him without fear; if God is our Father, he will not give us stones when we ask for bread. It should be noticed not only that these convictions are based on the projections of the model, but also that the model is action guiding. How shall we come to God? Without fear, because he is our Father. And the model is only action guiding in virtue of its claim to be reality depicting, namely, this is how it is with our relationship to God.[7]

The language used is, indeed, expressive of devotion, but that does nothing to show that it is lacking in cognitive content. Indeed, it shows the reverse, for the worshipper needs some conception of what the object of worship is like. In any case, as Richard Swinburne[8] has recently pointed out, not all language used of God is

---

[7] (Oxford University Press, 1985), 112.

[8] *Revelation: From Metaphor to Analogy* (Oxford: Clarendon Press, 1992).

metaphorical. Some expressions are literal or analogical as when we say that God knows everything or loves everyone. This is important because it provides a basic structure of metaphysical theory which can help us determine in what ways metaphors require to be qualified when applied to God. To be sure God does not know in the way we know—his knowledge is for the most part immediate and not inferential, but whatever can be known he knows it.

> The clever men at Oxford
> Know all that there is to be knowed,
> But none of them knows half as much
> As Intelligent Mr Toad.[9]

We have no difficulty in understanding, if not in crediting, the omniscience of the clever men at Oxford.

As for the second misconception, the notion that a precise decision-procedure is available in the sciences but not in theology has been no less influential. It has long been part of the stock-in-trade of empirically-minded philosophers; and theologians have often been prepared to accept it as affording them a licence to exploit existential decisions without rational constraint. But this sharp contrast too is increasingly difficult to maintain. There may be a strict decision-procedure available even in religion, as the case of a Lourdes miracle shows. There are very strict criteria laid down for what is to count as a miracle and, given the evidence in a particular case, a clear decision can generally be made by applying them carefully. But the procedure is

---

[9] See 'The Place of Symbols in Christianity', in Basil Mitchell, *How to Play Theological Ping-Pong* (London: Hodder & Stoughton, 1990).

able to operate only against a massive background of received doctrine which is not in the same way capable of being definitely decided. In science the area of the definitely decidable is, no doubt, somewhat greater, but, even in the natural sciences, there are larger, more controversial, questions in which the accepted answers are open to challenge and the individual scientist's decision has to be a matter of judgement.

Thus Newton-Smith emphasizes the importance of personal judgement in scientific work. After noting the inevitable absence of rules for the scientist's everyday perceptual judgements or for his skill in the design and execution of experiments, he goes on: 'On the account given of theory choice there is an even grander role to be played by judgement in science. For even if we do our best to pay attention to the relevant features, no clear verdict may be forthcoming. Reasonable men may be expected to have reasonable disagreements as to what to do in the circumstances. There is no knockdown proof of superiority at the time the choice has to be made.'[10] The pros and cons of Darwin's theory of natural selection at the time of the publication of *The Origin of Species* would afford a familiar example.

So far in this chapter I have attempted to show that the restrictions placed upon the exercise of reason by Hume and Kant are no longer appropriate to the scientific activity they were designed to fit, hence that, once freed from these restrictions, reason can and should be restored to the domain of religion from which they and many of their successors sought to expel it. The

10 Newton-Smith, *Rationality*, 234.

anti-rationalist tenor of theology after Schleiermacher traded upon a defective understanding of reason and was encouraged by it to pose a series of stark alternatives; not reason, but direct acquaintance or imagination or will was at the heart of Christian faith. In this it exemplified the spirit of the Romantic movement of which it was one important expression.

However, to make a fair judgement upon these theologians, it is not enough to show that they operated with an inadequate conception of reason: it is necessary to show that a more adequate conception would find a place for the other powers of the human mind to which they drew attention. In what remains of this chapter I shall endeavour to address this issue, and because of its central importance, I shall begin with the claim that faith in God is more a matter of direct acquaintance than of theoretical enquiry. As John Hick has so often reminded us, the great religious figures do not need to infer the existence of God from the existence and character of the world; they are directly aware of his abiding presence.

That knowledge of God is not merely a matter of detached theoretical enquiry but rather of direct encounter is a truth that we should be grateful to receive from Schleiermacher and the Romantic movement, but it does not in the least follow from this insight that there is no need for philosophical enquiry. Consider once again our awareness of persons. They are the most complex and problematic entities we have to do with, and yet in a straightforward sense our knowledge of them is immediate. But, in order to understand them, we need to approach them in two related ways. We need to attend carefully to the thoughts and feelings, the motives and intentions of individuals as expressed in language and in facial expression and in bodily behaviour; and we need to be able to interpret these in terms of conceptions of character and personality that are, so far as we can make them, coherent and defensible. However implicit and intuitive the first process may be, it cannot be divorced entirely from the second. The fact that our knowledge of persons is, for the most part, immediate and intuitive does not remove the need for theoretical concern with what it is to be a person.

Our understanding of people, whose inexhaustibility entails that our knowledge of them is never final or complete, provides the closest analogy we have to our knowledge of God; and if it is true that it relies on a critical awareness of all sorts of signs and clues, as well as a defensible conception of what it is to be a human being, so must our awareness of God depend on something comparable.

But, it may be objected, knowledge of this sort, whether it be knowledge of other persons or knowledge of God is bound up essentially with love and trust and, although the critical intellect may be involved in a subordinate role, that is a position that reason cannot consent to occupy so long as it is concerned, as it ought to be, with the pursuit of truth. Love of others and, even more so, love of God is entirely incompatible with an attitude of critical detachment.

If this is, indeed, the case we are in an awkward predicament in our attempts to know other people. The close concern with them and deep sympathy with them which is a necessary condition of coming to know them well would seem to invalidate any judgements we form about them. Rather, as if one could not judge the quality of wine without drinking enough of it to upset one's critical capacities altogether. But is the relationship between love and knowledge at all like this?

I happened quite recently to be reading some critical articles upon Jane Austen's *Emma*. There was a surprising degree of agreement among the critics that Emma's development throughout the novel is one of education through love. As one critic remarks: 'Emma's wisdom nearly ruins her happiness till she finds that wisdom is nothing unless it is directed by love.'[11] In the novel, Emma learns through her mistakes, and the process of learning is one in which she comes to see more clearly and judge more wisely in proportion as she is freed from self-centred pride. Her education is watched over by Knightley who has loved her all the time, but whose love for Emma, far from obscuring his clear vision of her errors, actually intensifies it.

This reciprocal relationship between knowledge and love can be expressed in other ways. Iris Murdoch puts it negatively and talks of 'the fat relentless ego' and how it distorts our apprehension of the good. In explicitly Christian language this is sin. That the human intellect is infected by sin, both individual and corporate, is a fundamental Christian insight which must correct any easy assumption about the self-sufficiency of reason. But terms like 'distort' and 'infect' presuppose a norm of clear vision and healthy functioning which must in

---

[11] Richard Simpson in David Lodge (ed.), *Jane Austen: a Selection of Critical Essays* (London: Macmillan, 1968), 56.

principle be capable of being restored if these terms are to retain their meaning.

Jane Austen is, of course, no Romantic, but it may be that her conception of the relation between love and knowledge can provide a clue to the role of the imagination and the will, to which the Romantics were so sensitive. Determinedly unromantic though Knightley is he comes to understand Emma better than she understands herself, and that involves a capacity on his part to imagine a range of different possible people that Emma might become and different choices she might make, and decide which of them represents her real vocation and which would enable her to flourish most fully. To be able to do this requires sensitivity to her real thoughts and feelings, but this too presupposes the ability to imagine possibilities and to choose between them: in other words, imagination. From the start he determines to trust her and in virtue of this he exerts his imagination to the full in order increasingly to understand her. But if, in the end, he is to judge wisely, his critical intellect has to be satisfied too. Otherwise how he is to tell that he understands her truly?

I suggested in the last chapter that 'if we start with the Christian revelation itself and what we are committed to by accepting it, there is no bar to the full exertion of our intellectual energies'. Trust in a person, and even more so, trust in God, engages the emotions, the imagination, and the will, because it engages the whole person and, by that same token, engages the intellect as well.

But this conclusion may only awaken a further misgiving. Surely, it may be objected following Barth, the notion of critical assessment is totally out of place in any phase of our relationship with God. Do I not seem to be saying that unaided human reason is able to penetrate the mysteries of God and even to sit in judgement on the word of God? To this I would reply. A delicate balance has to be struck. If it is true, as it clearly is, that we are not able to predict the creative discoveries of human genius by relying simply on some apparatus of theory antecedently available to us, it is true *a fortiori* that we cannot anticipate God's revelation of himself. Nevertheless, not everything that purports to be original discovery is actually such; we need to be persuaded that what the creative thinker offers us as a fresh truth does indeed illuminate what was previously obscure and does re-integrate it into a new and convincing pattern. And this is so, even though, as is likely to be the case, we may be dependent upon the creative thinker himself to engage and enhance our intellectual and imaginative capacities to the full, so that we can grasp the pattern and recognize its truth.

Similarly, not everything that purports to be revelation is to be accepted as such. Love of God must be love of *God* and, if in our total response to him, reason is still at work, its role is to sit in judgement not indeed on God, but on all that human ignorance or self-will seeks to substitute for God.

5

Faith and Rational Choice

I have argued that faith and criticism are two sides of one coin. Without faith in an established tradition criticism has nothing to fasten on; without criticism the tradition ceases in the end to have any purchase on reality. An important consequence follows from this which provides a secondary theme for this book. There is an inevitable tension between those who want above all to hold fast to traditional beliefs and make sure that nothing of value is lost even at the risk of a clash with 'modern knowledge'; and those who want above all to proclaim a faith that is relevant to our times even at the risk of sacrificing some elements of traditional doctrine. Both emphases are necessary and it is a tragedy for the Church that the two should so often be in uncomprehending conflict.

It would be natural to label these two parties 'conservatives' and 'liberals' but I have already reserved these expressions to mark the distinction between those who hold that Christian theology should be studied critically in the light of all the resources of modern scholarship and those who resist this trend as destructive of the historic faith of Christians. Judged by this criterion the two parties I have just characterized are both recognizably liberals—they both accept that the Christian tradition of faith is, in principle, open to criticism. The difference between them is that the one party is inclined to stress tradition, while the other emphasizes the claims of 'modern knowledge'. As regards the major distinction it is true of academic theologians that 'we are all liberals now'. That is why it was so important to show, as I have tried to show, that liberalism in that sense is not incompatible with whole-hearted faith. This means, however, that we need other terminology for the distinction we are now making and I propose to call them 'traditionalists' and 'progressives'.

If the difference between progressives and traditionalists is, as I am suggesting, merely one of emphasis, it may seem odd that there should be so much animus between them, but there are reasons why it should not surprise us:

(*a*) The questions at issue between them are of fundamental importance. However true it may be, in the abstract, that we need to hold on to what is essential in the faith and also to revise our interpretation of Christian doctrine where that is plainly necessary, it is far from easy to decide in practice just where the balance should be struck; and each party is subject to temptations which may gravely distort its judgement and, when it yields to them, incur the suspicion of the other. Progressives are, rightly, determined to rate at their true value the claims of modern thought, but there is continuous pressure upon them to assess these claims uncritically and, in so doing, to surrender to the ephemeral fashions of today or, more often, yesterday. This can often mean, in practice, embracing a 'scientific world-view' which is already out of date. Traditionalists, for their part, are often reluctant to address themselves to evidence that might threaten to disturb their convictions. While each party can see clearly the failings of the other, neither is, as a rule, aware of its own.

(*b*) It is a melancholy feature of church life, as any church periodical will show, that there is greater bitterness against opponents on one's own side than there is against those who are on the other side altogether. This is not, however, altogether surprising. It is natural for both parties to think of their common task as being that of defending a citadel against the secular forces which would invade it. They expect the enemy to attack it and accept this as a regrettable fact of life. But they expect their allies to defend it, and it is hard not to feel resentment when they are seen to yield up salients which they ought to be defending with their lives. It is equally exasperating to find one's allies using their precious resources to defend positions which anyone should see are indefensible, instead of straightening the perimeter along a line that can actually be held. Although in a cool hour both parties can appreciate that some modifications to the line are going to be necessary, they will not always agree as to how radical these should be, least of all in the heat of battle. Progressives fear that, when it comes to the point, traditionalists will insist on dying in the last ditch rather than make the needed changes; and traditionalists fear that the progressives will surrender the citadel to the enemy altogether.

(*c*) These fears are not totally unreasonable. Traditionalists can, under pressure, abandon their respect for reason and progressives can so modify the tradition that it ceases to be recognizably Christian. The first of these possibilities needs no further explanation; the second requires to be elaborated.

Underlying the whole discussion so far has been an assumption that in the debate between traditionalists and progressives a balance can in fact be struck. That is to say that the Christian tradition embodies a message of such a kind that it can retain its identity while subject to revision in the light of developing knowledge. If that is so, the task of the Christian theologian is to determine what the Church should believe now, given that the biblical writers and their successors in the Christian tradition believed what they did. It is assumed that this task, though enormously exacting, is in principle capable of fulfilment. What worries the traditionalists is that their liberal opponents might not actually believe that this is so, or, if they do believe it, might be forced by the logic of their argument to give up the belief.

This worry is not entirely without foundation. Even so moderate and thoughtful a progressive as Maurice Wiles lends some credence to this suspicion:

while our attempts to discover true doctrine must always be related to Jesus, there cannot be any external tests by which we can know whether we are doing the job rightly or not. . . . We have to go on with the hermeneutical task, trying to understand as fully as we can the scriptural witness to Jesus; we have to go on seeking to respond to God through him in prayer and worship. On the basis of all that, Christians have to say what seems to them to be true about God and his dealings with the world . . . The Spirit is sovereign and does not guarantee to underwrite even our most faithful and devoted undertakings. But, if we are working in the way I have outlined, and if we take seriously our own limitations and our own fallibility, we must then affirm what seems to us to be true. We have to take our stand there; we can do no other.[1]

There is much that is valuable in this, especially its emphasis on the role of judgement, but it suffers from a crucial ambiguity—the vagueness of the requirement that doctrine 'must always be related to Jesus'. Suppose, to take an extreme case, someone studies the New Testament in relation to its historical background, the teachings of the Fathers and the rest of the 'theological agenda', and concludes on the basis of these hermeneutical studies that the claims made for Jesus by the Church are without foundation. The enquiries of such a person are certainly 'related to Jesus' but they plainly do not represent Christian doctrine. 'We must affirm what seems to us to be true' is hopelessly subjective if our task is to define Christian doctrine. 'What seems to us to be true' might be no longer Christian.

There is perhaps an assumption underlying this passage from Wiles about what it would have to be like for contemporary doctrine to be a drawing out of the implications of biblical teaching. Wiles could be assuming that, if he were to think of it in this way, he would be committed to such claims as the following:

(1) that doctrine in the New Testament forms an entirely consistent system

[1] *The Remaking of Christian Doctrine* (London: SCM Press, 1974), 13–14.

(2) that it represents a set of entirely clear and distinct ideas

(3) that all of it, as it stands, is true.

These claims he rightly believes to be erroneous. It is interesting to notice that they are in fact close to the claims that a biblical fundamentalist would make. One would only need to add:

— that all of it is to be interpreted, so far as possible, as being literally true.

Since Wiles cannot, in all intellectual honesty, accept these claims, he feels bound to adopt what appears to him to be the only available alternative, viz. the entirely open-ended activity that he identifies with hermeneutics.

But, surely, this is not the only alternative. It might be the case that, although the New Testament does not contain a set of entirely consistent teachings, ready-made, so to speak, it does nevertheless possess an overall coherence which becomes steadily more apparent the more it is studied and meditated upon. This would be likely to be so if its message was often couched in the language of analogy and metaphor whose meaning is inherently inexhaustible—capable of being applied to many different cultural situations and interpreted in terms of a variety of philosophical concepts. If this were so, it would not, indeed, be possible for Christian thinkers at any given time in history to predict just how a particular doctrine would be interpreted, and rightly interpreted, at some future period, but it would be possible to distinguish, at that later period, between what was a genuine development of the original message and what was a corruption or dilution of it. And this surely is the case. And this being the case, of course there is no simple set of rules by which such a discrimination can be made, and in that sense, there is no guarantee of correctness—here Wiles is entirely right—but, as we have seen, the same is true in any important sphere of human enquiry. It is essential to distinguish between two assertions:

(*a*) If theology is a creative discipline, it is not possible at any time to predict what fresh and genuine insights later theologians may achieve into the nature of Christian truth.

(*b*) Any conclusions which later theologians may arrive at after considering the relevant evidence will represent a fresh and genuine insight into Christian doctrine.

The first of these assertions is plainly true, the second obviously false. The point is entirely general where interpretation is concerned. We cannot now predict what further depths of meaning future interpreters of Shakespeare will, rightly, find in *Hamlet* or *King Lear*. It does not follow that whatever claims future scholars or theatrical directors make as to Shakespeare's meaning will in fact be justified.

With this distinction in mind it will be instructive to look at a more recent description by Wiles of the traditionalist/progressive divide, in which it is implicitly recognized. It is to be found in the concluding paragraph of his contribution to *The Oxford Illustrated History of Christianity*. After describing certain contemporary influences upon Christian belief he writes:

For some the impact such developments have already had is seen as a form of betrayal. The rallying-call is to a greater faithfulness to past tradition, to some form of that 'common stock of belief' I have been trying to describe. Perhaps that way will find itself at home in a future post-Enlightenment culture. But it seems more likely to lead in the direction of a Christian ghetto, Christian belief as a minority option clearly seen to be incompatible with the main stream of understanding of the world. For others the need for further change in the forms of Christian belief seems self-evident, however uncertain they may be of the precise direction in which it may lead. For them what Christians believe today remains a crucial guide to life and truth, but it has a necessary provisionality about it. What such people hold is perhaps less a clear-cut system of belief than a conviction that the resources of scripture and the Christian tradition will continue to inform a way of believing in God through Jesus Christ which will be consistent with our changing understanding of the world.[2]

This captures very well how the contending parties see their differences. It prompts one to ask what, if anything, it is that they have in common. I take it to be this: They both seek to adhere to that interpretation of Christian doctrine which would best reflect the Christian message in the light of the full tradition of the Church and whatever knowledge is now available to us which might further illuminate it. It is not to be expected, given the limitations of the human mind and the transcendent nature of the final truth, that we should capture it fully, but we have been given reason to believe that it is not wholly beyond our grasp. As Wiles says, what Christians believe today remains a crucial guide, together

[2] In J. McManners (ed.), *The Oxford Illustrated History of Christianity* (Oxford University Press, 1990), 571.

with what they have believed in the past (and may be overlooking today), but it cannot be regarded as entirely definitive. Traditionalists will typically stress the need to adhere to traditional formulations unless and until something plainly better is forthcoming which can be shown to represent more adequately what the tradition was trying to say. Progressives will typically judge the tradition to be less coherent and more in need of revision; they will be more adventurous as they seek to learn lessons from contemporary thought and experience. To put it in another way; both sides want the truth. Traditionalists are concerned above all to maintain those truths which we already possess, embodied in a tradition we have learned to trust; progressives seek new truths, or new interpretations of old truths. So long as both see themselves as engaged in this joint quest their disagreements are necessary and fruitful. They err if they abandon either element in the quest. 'It takes all the running you can do to keep in the same place.' It is a mistake to think you can stay in the same place without running, but it is also a mistake to go on running regardless of what place you find yourself in.

But there is a yet more radical critique of this whole way of considering the matter which we must now confront. I have assumed, and have just now reiterated, that both traditionalists and progressives are concerned with truth; and I have argued that the tension between faith and criticism makes for a fuller understanding of truth. The tradition embodies truth, albeit incompletely, essentially the same truth as was originally revealed. Criticism is founded upon the discovery of new truths which need to be understood and assimilated. But there is an influential movement, in theology as elsewhere, in terms of which the hermeneutic task of restating the Christian message as found in the biblical writers and their successors today in the Christian tradition is altogether impossible of fulfilment. According to their view such is the gulf which lies between the thought forms of these ancient writers and our own that, even if by an enormous effort of the imagination we could manage to understand what they said, there is no possibility of our assenting to it. The most that we can achieve—and it is all that we need to achieve—is that through our involvement with that continuing institution, the Church, we have the same relationship with God now as was enjoyed by Christians in previous centuries, although inevitably we conceptualize that relationship in a way that is radically different.

It is tempting to reject this view out of hand by a simple appeal to experience. Generation upon generation of Christian believers, not excluding our own, have nurtured themselves upon the Bible and used its language to express their deepest thoughts and feelings. For many, it is more readily understood and assented to than are most contemporary writers. Similarly those of us who have had occasion to study the Greek and Roman classics have often found them to contain the most memorable expressions of truths about the human condition. Hence the tendency of philosophers to point to certain passages of, say, Plato or Aristotle as containing the 'classical formulation' of a well-known problem. Some years ago I went for a walk with a theological friend in Christ Church meadow in Oxford, in the course of which he insisted upon the impossibility of our now grasping the thought forms of St Paul—such was the gulf between ourselves and the first century AD. Later, at lunch, I found myself sitting next to a colleague, a distinguished philosophical scholar, and I took the opportunity of asking him (without disclosing my motive for doing so) whether in his view Aristotle had said anything that was both true and important. He was, I think, rather surprised at the question, but he answered without hesitation. 'Oh yes certainly, most of what he said about the foundations of logic and a lot of what he said about the relation between moral character and moral discernment.'

All that this shows, it may be said, is that philosophers are more credulous than theologians—a phenomenon I have noticed upon other occasions. And there are, of course, philosophers who embrace the conceptual relativism that has influenced some radical theologians. Confronted by the common sense rejoinders that I have mentioned they argue that, when one is under the impression that one is understanding and assenting to beliefs that originated in another culture, one is being misled. What is actually happening is that one is interpreting them in terms of one's own culture without being aware of the scale of the transformation that is taking place. The philosophical student of Aristotle may suppose that he is able to some extent to think the thoughts of Aristotle and to adapt them to his own use, but that impression ceases to be plausible as soon as account is taken of the very different assumptions that governed Aristotle's thought, embedded as they were in a very different social and cultural situation from our own.

If there is force in this critique it is obvious that the line I have been taking in this book is peculiarly vulnerable to it. For I have emphasized the centrality in human life of world-views and philosophies of life, and stressed the extent to which they rely on a continuing tradition. I have taken it for granted throughout that they are capable of rational assessment. If this relativist critique is right, not only is there no possibility of making a rational choice between world-views, but the claims of a given world-view to a logical as well as a merely historical continuity with thinkers in the past are without foundation. To discuss, as I have done, what should be the response of faith to criticism is to assume that criticism is able to get a purchase on faith as if it had some independent authority of its own—a naive assumption to make in a post-modern age.

The relativist critique purports to show that there could not be any way of achieving a rational decision between large-scale systems of the sort we have in mind. The argument is that, for such decision to be possible, one would need prior agreement between the parties as to the data of observation and as to the principles of rationality to be appealed to in the debate; and this is not to be had. For it is characteristic of such systems that each one of them determines for itself what is to count as evidence and what are to function as the basic principles of rationality. As proponents of this argument are fond of putting it, 'we have no neutral ground on which to stand'.

It is important to realize that this problem, if it arises at all, arises also in relation to scientific theories, and it is in this context indeed that it has been most intensively studied. And here too it arises not only when comparisons are attempted between rival theories, but equally between successive stages of the same theory. Thus, if the meaning of a theoretical term such as 'electron' or 'gene' is defined by reference to a particular theory, and if this meaning determines what it is that is being talked about when the term is used, it follows that, should the theory be modified, the term, as now defined by the revised theory, no longer refers to the same entity as the term originally did, defined as it then was by an earlier and strictly incompatible theory. Hence when, as we should naturally say, it was discovered that genes were bearers of inherited characteristics and not, as was thought when the term was first introduced, of acquired characteristics, our way of speaking is erroneous, for we are no longer talking of the same thing. (I take this example from Janet Martin Soskice.)[3] What appear to be disagreements are no longer so; the subject has changed.

The consequences of accepting this thesis are so manifestly absurd that one is bound to examine the credentials of the theory of meaning and reference upon which it rests and look for a more acceptable one: one, that is, which will allow us to agree as to what it is we are talking about without our having to be tied down to some specific description of it which cannot subsequently be varied.

The most promising theory known to me is one which stresses the part played in securing reference to unobservable entities by such expressions as 'that which causes'

---

[3] *Metaphor*, 131.

certain agreed effects, together with models and metaphors whose nature it is to be inherently revisable. Hence, as Janet Soskice puts it in a persuasive development of this theme:

Terms like 'gene' are introduced with fixed senses (say, 'the mechanism responsible for the inheritance of acquired characteristics') but this sense, while guiding investigations, does not necessarily determine what it is that, in practice, the term is used to refer to. As the theory is improved, the original sense of the term may be altered (say, by deleting 'acquired') or in some cases (e.g. 'phlogiston') it may be decided that a term fails to refer at all. So the sense of the terms is important, not in tying one to a direct and exhaustive description of the referent, but rather in providing access to a referent, which access it is then the task of science to refine.[4]

Once one has abandoned the assumption that the meaning of theoretical terms is tied to particular theories, the main ground for denying that rival theories can be rationally compared collapses. And the benefit of this finding is available to theology as well. Reference to God can be secured by thinking of him as 'that which causes the universe to exist' or 'that which caused some archetypal religious experience' and the resources of metaphor and analogy can be drawn upon to develop a theological system which can then be criticized and compared with others.

The philosophical objector may, perhaps, still insist that principles of rationality also vary as between one system and another, and this makes rational comparison impossible. Since the argument so far has been somewhat

[4] Ibid.

abstract, let me invoke an experience, that of discussing a difficult and profound issue with a sympathetic critic who does not share one's fundamental beliefs about it. I recall particularly a wide-ranging conversation I had one evening in my room in Oxford with a Hindu philosopher, who sometimes understood my position even better than I did myself. The test of his comprehension was that he would say from time to time: 'I am surprised to hear you say that. I should have thought that, from your point of view, you would have said something more like this . . .' and he would then go on to develop 'my' position in directions I had not thought of but acknowledged to be right.

Now it could, perhaps, be objected that this individual's capacity to think my thoughts with me, and even for me, is consistent with there being nevertheless an impermeable barrier between his system of belief and mine of such a kind that, although we can each reason within our own and, given enough empathy, within each other's, there is no possibility of our judging between them, even if it seems to us that this is just what we are successfully doing.

In a thoughtful discussion of this issue Alasdair MacIntyre states the problem thus: 'Our education in and about philosophy has by and large presupposed what is in fact not true, that there are standards of rationality, adequate for the evaluation of rival answers to such questions, equally available, at least in principle, to all persons, whatever tradition they happen to find themselves in and whether or not they inhabit any tradition.' But he insists that 'genuine intellectual encounter does not and cannot take place in some generalized abstract way'. Rather, a person who is at home in a particular tradition can and should engage 'both in the ongoing arguments within that tradition and in the argumentative debates and conflicts of that tradition of enquiry with one or more of its rivals.'[5] This, of course, is precisely what my Hindu friend and I were doing and I wholeheartedly agree with MacIntyre that it is both necessary and possible, though I confess that I do not see how this recommendation (or, indeed, the experience of having to all appearance followed it successfully) enables us to meet the original criticism if, indeed, it has any weight. For the critic is not denying that we sometimes have the subjective impression of understanding and assenting to assertions that are made within a tradition other than our own: he is insisting that, notwithstanding this impression, we cannot (logically cannot) actually be doing so.

The reason given is that the claim that we are doing so presupposes that there are standards of rationality neutral between the rival traditions by reference to which their claims can be assessed. 'In short,' to quote Lindbeck, 'religions like languages can be understood only in their own terms, not by transposing them into an alien speech.'[6]

What is it, then, that we cannot do, but if only we could do it, would make rational assessment of competing claims possible? Lindbeck, with his linguistic analogy, makes it sound as if what we need to be able to

[5] *Whose Justice? Which Rationality?* (London: Duckworth, 1988), 393–4.
[6] George Lindbeck, *The Nature of Doctrine* (London: SPCK, 1984), 129.

do, but cannot do, is find a language—say, Esperanto—which is such that everyone can speak it well without having to learn it. If and only if we can find such a language will it be possible to translate, say, from English into German by dint of first translating both into Esperanto. The notion, however, is ridiculous—we can and do translate from English into German directly once we have learnt both languages.

The linguistic analogy, then, does not help. Let us abandon it and remember that it is *standards of rationality* that are in question. The claim is that unless there exist framework-independent standards of rationality we cannot adjudicate between traditions; and there are no framework-independent standards of rationality.

Supposing we had framework-independent standards of rationality, what would they be like? The natural answer is that they would be principles of deductive and inductive logic as set forth in logic textbooks and that we do in fact have them. However, if there is, indeed, a problem about rational comparison between rival traditions, this does not provide a solution to it. For when faced by difficult questions within a particular tradition like, for example, the problem within the Christian tradition of how to interpret the Resurrection, formal logic, whether deductive or inductive, provides only very limited assistance. To be sure, we must reject an interpretation of the Resurrection which involves a contradiction but whether it involves a contradiction to say that Christ's risen body appeared at the same time in different places depends upon how one conceives that body, which in turn depends upon the historical evidence for the Resurrection which, as we saw earlier, cannot be assessed independently of the metaphysical beliefs of the interpreters. Elements in the argument can no doubt be expressed in terms of Bayes's theorem as an exercise in inductive logic, but the argument as a whole cannot be formalized. So we are led to say not 'Only if there were framework-independent standards of rationality could we engage in arguments of this sort' but rather 'Even if there were framework-independent standards of rationality, they would not suffice for arguments of this sort.'

What happens when reliance is placed upon standards readily available to all is well stated by Newman:

When we come to what is called Evidence, or in popular language, exercises of Reason, prejudice and mental peculiarities are excluded from the discussion; we descend to grounds common to all; certain scientific rules and fixed standards for weighing testimony and examining facts are received. Nothing can be urged, or made to tell, but what all feel, all comprehend, all can put into words; current language becomes the meaning of thought; only such conclusions may be drawn as can produce their reasons; only such reasons are in point as can be exhibited in simple propositions; the multiform and intricate assemblage of considerations which really lead to judgement and action must be attenuated or mutilated into a major and a minor premise.[7]

Lindbeck finally arrives at a position close to Newman's: 'The norms of reasonableness are too rich and subtle to be adequately specified in any general theory of reason or knowledge,'[8]—though it is not clear how far he realizes that this provides the solution to his

[7] *University Sermons*, 229.   [8] *Nature of Doctrine*, 130.

problem. The demand that, for adherents of rival world-views to understand one another they must be able to specify the principles of rationality upon which they rely, is an altogether unreasonable one.

If this is so, there does not after all seem to be any good reason why my conversation with the Hindu philosopher should not be what it appeared to both of us to be, viz. a dialogue in which to a very large extent we each understood what the other was saying and appreciated the force of the arguments the other was using. To be sure, our mutual comprehension was helped by the fact that he had studied Western analytic philosophy under Strawson and I had studied, though less intensively, Hindu philosophy under Radhakrishnan. But, surely, no-one, not even a philosopher, could suppose that people can come to understand subtle and complex schemes of thought without learning the necessary skills. In any case it is obvious that how well individuals are able to do this depends not only upon training but also upon natural endowments of empathy and imagination. People vary enormously in this respect, which is why some people are, and others are not, good teachers.

The best teacher I ever came across was H. H. Price.[9] Those who knew him will remember that he was a very shy man who habitually, when talking or listening, fixed his gaze upon an upper corner of the room—unless there was some image of an owl or cat available. It would happen from time to time in his informal classes that I would make a rather muddled contribution to the

---

[9] Wykeham Professor of Logic, Oxford University, 1935–59.

discussion, whereupon, after a moment's pause for reflection he would reply, 'Yes. I wonder whether *this* would represent what you want to say,' and there would follow a carefully articulated sentence having the following characteristics: (a) it was clear, (b) it was, so far as one could tell, true, (c) it was recognizably what one was trying to say.

In this way Price provided a small face-to-face example of the hermeneutic process whose possibility in principle we were considering earlier in this chapter, the process by which a philosophical scholar may conjecture what Aristotle was trying to say or a biblical scholar what St Paul was trying to say and set it out in terms defensible today.

A further consideration is this: It is assumed by all parties that traditions of thought are capable of development. How do they develop? Presumably by encountering objections and taking steps to meet them. But where do the objections come from if not from facts and well-founded theories not at present catered for in the tradition itself? To be registered as objections, the facts must be acknowledged as facts (and *a fortiori* the propositions asserting them must be acknowledged as intelligible); and the theories must be recognized as coherent and well-evidenced. If this is so, then *either*:

(*a*) The facts and theories which are acknowledged as valid objections are embedded in some rival tradition of thought, and the incommensurability thesis breaks down at once;

or (*b*) They are tradition-independent and require to be taken account of (and can be taken account of) by any tradition which seeks to be comprehensive.

In the light of this discussion, we are in a position to reject the relativistic claim that the differences between past thought forms and our own are such that the scholar's task is inherently impossible of fulfilment. It follows that the hermeneutic task, difficult though it is, can be carried out more or less successfully. How successfully will be a matter of judgement, and the degree of success achievable will depend on the intrinsic difficulty of different elements in the task as well as the skill and sensitivity of those engaged in it.

In the execution of this task, both traditionalists and progressives have an essential part to play. The continuous tension between them is an inevitable condition of progress, where progress consists in the achievement at any given time of as full an approximation to the truth as the circumstances of that time allow.

6

Christian Ethics: Traditionalists and Progressives

Our previous argument has generated two main conclusions:

(*a*) The characteristically modern predicament is that of having to choose between alternative philosophies of life, knowing that a plausible case can be made against whichever one chooses. Nevertheless it is both necessary and possible to persevere in the chosen path with confidence and conviction.

(*b*) Typically, this involves adherence to a tradition. Within the tradition there is inevitably a tension between traditionalists and progressives. The former are concerned above all to ensure that nothing of value in the tradition is lost; the latter to test the tradition in terms of contemporary thought and experience. Neither party suffices on its own to maintain the tradition in a satisfactory state. In the case of Christianity, there are both philosophical and historical reasons why this should be so. Religious language and symbolism are needed to capture its truth, but cannot capture it definitively once and for all in such a way that it needs no further interpretation; hence, in the course of

Christian history there are plenty of instances in which interpretations, once accepted, have later been abandoned. Tradition, although an indispensable guide to truth, is not an infallible, nor even an indefectible one. It is even more obvious that a progressive stance alone will not suffice. Once cut off from the tradition it rapidly becomes indistinguishable from the secular culture of the day.

If all this is true of doctrine, it is even more evidently true of morality. The modern individual is faced with a plurality of moral standpoints and has no alternative but to choose between them or to behave as if he had chosen. Whereas there is, at least in theory, the option of suspending judgement so far as one's overall philosophy of life is concerned, this is not possible with morality. Hence Descartes, when he embarked upon his project of systematic doubt, explicitly excepted the principles of morality from its operation.

The problem of faith and criticism must, then, arise with particular severity in the moral case. Whatever morality we as individuals embrace will be open to criticism from the supporters of rival positions. If we take these criticisms seriously, so the argument runs, our adherence to our own moral principles will be tentative and provisional. If we are to display whole-hearted conviction in our. moral life, we must reject the possibility of criticism.

There are two ways of denying, nevertheless, that the problem does in fact arise in relation to ethics; one no longer at all common, the other all too prevalent. It has often been remarked that the Victorians, although racked with doubts about Christian doctrine, took

Christian ethics entirely for granted—to such an extent, indeed, that they tended to identify them with ethics as such. Until recently it was still possible to maintain that, however much in this country we might differ about religious or ideological questions, we agreed fundamentally about morality. A generation or two ago it was natural for moralists like Sir David Ross to regard as intuitively self-evident moral principles which have subsequently been characterized as simply those of a Christian English gentleman. I myself remember that, when I first started to teach moral philosophy, I could reckon to test moral theories, as Ross himself did, by getting pupils to agree as to what one ought to do in a particular situation, and then asking whether the moral theory in question would, when applied to that situation, yield the required judgement. It became in time increasingly difficult to use this procedure: there simply was no longer the implied consensus about particular cases.

Our present situation is typified, rather, by the work of Peter Singer[1] who launches an all-out attack upon the Western ethical tradition, which he sees as having been infected with illegitimate—and, in his view, indefensible—Christian assumptions. A similar, albeit more moderately expressed, critique is to be found in the writings of the late J. L. Mackie.[2]

This frank recognition that much of our traditional morality is based on Christian assumptions and that different metaphysical presuppositions would yield a

---

[1] See, for example, Helga Kuhse and Peter Singer, *Should the Baby Live?* (Oxford: Oxford University Press, 1985) Chapter 6.
[2] See *Ethics: Inventing Right and Wrong* (London: Penguin, 1977).

radically different approach to ethics, is now wide-spread, at least among intellectuals. Mackie and Singer, rightly in my view, regard the issue as one to be argued about. They both think that, as a philosophy of life, metaphysical materialism is more convincing than Christian theism and are prepared to argue for it and draw out its moral implications.

But, as we saw in the last chapter, an even more fashionable move is to claim that the rival systems are incommensurable. To be sure, materialism is incompatible with Christianity as it is also with Hinduism or New Age pantheism, but there is no question, even in principle, let alone in practice, of making a rational choice between them. Hence, the problem I have been addressing in this book altogether fails of application. Whether one is a Christian or a materialist or whatever other position one adopts, there is no requirement to take account of criticism, because any conceivable critic necessarily takes his stand upon some alternative position which is justifiable only in its own terms.

It is often claimed, further, that to view matters in this way is morally preferable because it makes for toleration. If one believes that there is an objective truth of the matter—and in the field of ethics an objective right and wrong—a conviction of one's own rightness is bound to result in one's denying to others the right to express, or even to hold, divergent opinions.

In point of fact it is the denial of objectivity that threatens toleration in modern—or should I say post-modern?—times. Hence Alasdair Macintyre calls attention to the phenomenon of protest:

It is easy . . . to understand why protest becomes a distinctive moral feature of the modern age and why indignation is a predominant modern emotion. . . . The self-assertive shrillness of protest arises because the facts of incommensurability ensure that protestors can never win an argument; the indignant self-righteousness of protest arises because the facts of incommensurability ensure equally that the protestors can never lose an argument either. Hence the utterance of protest is characteristically addressed to those who already share the protestors' premises.[3]

But since, in practical politics, you need to win your case, you have to use non-rational means of persuasion, including, increasingly, censorship. What is not 'politically correct' may not be uttered.

It was John Stuart Mill who saw most clearly the fallacy in the argument that objectivity implies the suppression of dissent: 'We can never be sure that the opinion we are endeavouring to stifle is a false opinion; and, if we were sure, stifling it would be an evil still.'[4] For, even if the received opinion were the whole truth of the matter, if other opinions were suppressed it would be likely to be held as an unreasoning prejudice and so would lose 'its vital effect on the character and conduct'. In speaking of 'the vital effect on character and conduct', Mill recognizes that a reasoned conviction, even if it is held in the face of criticism—indeed because it is so held—'informs the character' in such a way as to make it steadfast and unshakeable. It is a mark of insensitivity, not strength of character, to ignore or fail to notice serious criticisms of one's moral convictions.

[3] *After Virtue* (London: Duckworth, 1981), 68–9.
[4] *Essay on Liberty* (London: Everyman, 1910), 79.

Of course, prudence is required. There are times when it is above all necessary to resist temptation and it is wise, like Odysseus, to be tied securely to the mast while passing within earshot of the Sirens' voices. If one is in danger of being seduced, it is as well for the time being not to entertain arguments justifying occasional adultery. But it will not do as an overall policy to ignore criticism. Not only, as Mill saw, does one increasingly get cut off from the world as it is, but as a policy it cannot in the long run guarantee the strength and solidity claimed for it. The time will come when it will fracture under pressures which a more flexible position would be able to contain. To revert to the metaphor of the citadel, that line is best defended which can be modified where necessary to enhance the natural advantages which the citadel possesses.

That the tension between traditionalists and progressives is to be found in the sphere of morals is evident; and it is the cause of much anxiety and distress. The findings of a church report on some question of personal or social ethics are as a rule attacked from both sides. Traditionalists will examine the conclusions closely for indications that the authors have abandoned the traditional absolutes which ought to have guided their thinking. Progressives study the document with equal care to ascertain how far the authors have progressed towards the enlightened solutions which have long been apparent to all unprejudiced observers.

In any particular case, the critics may be right. The working party, in pursuit of an Anglican *via media*, may indeed have avoided extreme positions without following any logical path between them. It is a mistake to suppose that what it ought to be doing is to secure a compromise between Christian tradition as at present understood and the current trends of secular thought. The Christian message for today may not be—indeed generally will not be—exemplified straightforwardly in either position or in any compromise between them. The truth of the matter is well set out in one such report. In *Personal Origins*, a commentary on the Warnock Report prepared by a group set up by the Church of England Board for Social Responsibility, the authors remark that, in the new situation which faces us 'our traditions of moral thought need to be extended and rethought'.[5]

Both traditionalists and progressives are often in practice unwilling to accept this conclusion. Traditionalists, increasingly aware of the gap that is opening up between Christian and secular ethics, are suspicious of what seem to them to be attempts to accommodate Christian principles to secular modes of thought. Progressives tend to associate any talk of 'tradition' with an unwillingness to take account of new knowledge and fresh experience.

Both emphases are necessary and the tension between them is inevitable and salutary, though in practice, all too often, the suspicions which both parties entertain of the other are justified by their actual behaviour. Progressives are seduced by the attractions of secular thought into repudiating the claims of tradition altogether and, in response, traditionalists retreat into simple fundamentalism.

---

[5] (London: Church Information Office, 1985), 13, 41.

The situation can be illustrated by reference to the topic which the Warnock Report was concerned with, viz. the moral issues raised by *in vitro* fertilization. From a typically modern secular point of view there is no problem. If a couple want children they may reasonably use any methods on offer which will give them what they want, subject only to a calculation of possible consequences. Nor is there any need to restrict the availability of such techniques to 'couples' as that expression would normally be understood. If a woman wants children she may dispense with the partnership of a man altogether, except in the attenuated manner afforded by Artificial Insemination by Donor (AID). Or a homosexual couple of either sex may use such methods to procure a child whom they will raise together. There may, indeed, be objections, some of them quite weighty, to these arrangements but they are essentially of a utilitarian kind having to do mainly with the social disadvantages the child might suffer, given conventional attitudes.

There are some people, of course, who do find the new procedures problematic but not on explicitly Christian grounds. Their position, too, can be called 'secular', although it is open fairly obviously to Singer's critique as deriving from unavowed Christian pre-suppositions.[6]

[6] I am not happy myself with the simple dichotomy between Christian and secular standpoints. Not only do the moral intuitions of people in a partly secularized society reflect Christian assumptions but individuals often have a capacity for moral insight which is largely independent of religious influences. There are, I think, Christian reasons why this should be so, but I cannot go into them now. See my *Morality: Religious and Secular* (Oxford University Press, 1980), 160–1.

From a traditional Christian point of view the entire discussion about the acceptability of the techniques made possible by *in vitro* fertilization turns on the need to hold together the 'procreative' and the 'unitive' ends of marriage, where an 'end' is not a goal which we happen to choose, whose value for us depends upon our choosing it but, as the Report puts it 'a good which is part of the order of things and something which we discern by our reason and accept as part of the given nature of the way things are meant to be. Christians think of these "goods" as the creator's purpose for what he has made.'[7]

Given this traditional view of the relationship between marriage and procreation the question arises whether the new techniques can be regarded as assisting the ends of marriage or not. The difficult cases are those of AID, ovum donation and embryo donation, in which genetic material is introduced from outside the union altogether. Where there is some impediment to the union of sperm and ovum through normal sexual intercourse, and the husband's sperm is used, it would seem to be an entirely unobjectionable procedure to introduce some artificial intermediary.[8]

It is worth noting that the Warnock Report itself is not wholly clear in its attitude to this question. It is

---

[7] Personal Origins, 101, 36.

[8] The official Roman Catholic position, as set out in *Humanae Vitae* and *Veritatis Splendor* is more restrictive in its insistence that each and every act of intercourse must be 'open to procreation'. I do not think that the relevant principle of holding together the procreative and unitive ends of marriage requires this restriction.

prepared to accept AID in spite of the objection that 'it represents the introduction of a third party into what ought to be an exclusive relationship', but it discourages surrogate motherhood because, among other things, 'the moral and social objections to surrogacy weighed heavily with us'. Prominent among these, as stated in the Report, was that 'to introduce a third party into the process of procreation which should be confined to the loving partnership between two people, is an attack on the value of the marital relationship'. When I complained to Baroness Warnock that the Report set out the possible arguments for and against their proposals without indicating which of them had actually persuaded the Committee, she replied, with an air of resignation, that it was difficult enough to get agreement on the proposals, let alone on the reasons for them!

Given that the Warnock Committee did attach significance to this particular argument, one wonders why they allowed it to count against surrogacy but not against AID. This may have been due to a consideration which is also voiced in *Personal Origins*. The majority of the committee in that case ruled against AID for the reason given—that it represents the introduction of a third party into what ought to be an exclusive relationship—but a minority, while not denying that it represented a deviation from what ought to be the norm, nevertheless thought that, where a couple desire children and could not otherwise have them, a loving family made possible in this way is closer to the norm than is a marriage in which the desire for children is altogether frustrated. In so arguing, they illustrate a way in which a progressive attitude may seek to modify a traditional position, without altogether repudiating the principle upon which it rests.

This particular example of *in vitro* fertilization illustrates a pattern of disagreement which is discernible in all debates between Christian and secular moralists, at least typically modern ones. There is, on the Christian side, an underlying concern with an order of things which is somehow given, whose integrity human beings ought not to impair. In its most general sense this implies, as John Mackie put it in a sympathetic critique of it, that morality is 'required by the universe'.[9] Its Christian formulation has been in terms of 'Natural Law' or 'Orders of Creation', the one term current in Catholic, the other in Protestant theology. It involves the idea that there are built-in limits to what human individuals or societies may legitimately do in pursuit of their own aims. Where the limits should be drawn is a matter for argument, but that they should be drawn somewhere is taken for granted.

In talking up till now about a contrast between Christian and secular ethics, I have expressed myself loosely. The idea that morality is 'required by the universe' has in fact been shared by all systems of classical ethics, including those of classical antiquity and the other theistic religions. It is also shared to some degree by some contemporary movements of thought which do not always acknowledge its Christian associations, such as the environmental movement with its strong protest against the technological imperative— 'can' implies 'ought'—and its deep sense of the integrity

[9] *Ethics*, ch. 10.

of the natural world. Since it is of the essence of Environmentalism to insist that human beings are not free to interfere with the patterns of natural life simply to forward their own interests, this is an ethical imperative which is not readily thought of as the expression merely of human preferences. It requires that the claims of human autonomy be subordinated not to the preferences of the non-human world, for it has none, but to the needs of the natural order. As the environmental movement shows, there are in the modern world varieties of secular ethics and it is a mistake to lump them all together. There are, however, two dominant trends, each of which is in conflict with the Christian tradition and with the tenor of classical ethics.

One is utilitarian—a strain of causalism or consequentialism—which is suspicious of principles and is concerned solely with outcomes. From this standpoint, there is no such thing as sexual morality in the traditional sense of the sort that generates problems about *in vitro* fertilization. People are free to express their sexuality in any way they like subject only to conventions designed to avoid exploitation and undesirable consequences such as the birth of unwanted children. It is not denied that some individuals may have 'moral preferences' in favour of fidelity in sexual relationships, but these are essentially personal and have no authority beyond the decisions of those who adopt them. The interests of children must be taken account of but are to be judged solely in terms of their physical and psychological health. Hence, for example, there is no intrinsic evil in pornography; it is to be condemned only in so far as it can be shown to lead to undesirable consequences such as increased violence or other kinds of physical or psychological harm. Claims that in itself it exhibits a distorted form of sexual relationship and hence corrupts those who produce it and those who indulge in it are dismissed as 'moralistic'. The other is whât Alasdair Macintyre in *After Virtue* calls 'emotivism'. 'Emotivism is the doctrine that all evaluative judgements and more specifically all moral judgements are *nothing but* expressions of preference, expressions of attitude or feeling, in so far as they are moral or evaluative in character.'[10] Macintyre himself, as quoted earlier, calls attention to the peculiar shrillness of protest which results from the fact that, on this view, there is no possibility of making a rational choice between rival moralities.

As a rule, some sort of accommodation is attempted between these two strains in secular morality. The commonest is by way of distinguishing between public and private morality—the former utilitarian and open to rational discussion, the latter subjective and a matter for decision by individuals or voluntary groups. People get used to modulating between these two standpoints. But it is significant that, increasingly, this sort of accommodation is coming under strain. Feminist thinkers, for example, are for the most part not willing to have their objections to pornography dismissed as merely personal preferences to be confined to a private sphere. They complain (with good reason) that much pornography degrades women and corrupts the public perception of

[10] *After Virtue*, 11. Non-cognitivism is a more accurate term. R. M. Hare, its leading exponent, insists that moral judgements express imperatives.

them, whether or not it can be shown to cause physical or psychological harm; and they insist that this is a matter of public concern as affecting the entire ethos of society. They differ from Mary Whitehouse only in not objecting to representations of explicit sex as such. Indeed, one may generalize and say that the moral 'protests' to which Macintyre called attention ten years ago now take the form of more or less coherent ideologies whose proponents are increasingly vocal in the public arena. One consequence is that although almost everyone pays lip service to freedom of expression and repudiates censorship, very few—with the possible exception of Bernard Levin—are consistently against censorship in practice. It depends entirely on whose views are to be censored.

In so far, then, as Christians of a liberal temper are anxious to ensure that Christian ethics takes proper account of contemporary thought and experience, they will want the churches to engage in serious dialogue with such movements. They will wish to be alert for signs that God is speaking to us through them. They do not, as a rule, identify themselves entirely with these secular viewpoints, but rather try to see them as reflecting, albeit inadequately, certain genuine insights to which the Church ought to respond and which are, arguably, anticipated in the Christian tradition itself. They will stress the creativity and spontaneity of life in the Spirit, which is not bound by any conception of Natural Law. In matters of life and death they will stress the quality of life as against its mere continuation; and in sexual relationships they will place the emphasis not upon the nature of the acts performed but upon their capacity to express and confirm genuine love between the partners.

Traditionalists view these tendencies with alarm, and see in them the seeds of apostasy. The churches are being invited to abandon truths which have been accepted for centuries and which cannot be supposed to change over time. They resolve to close ranks and repudiate the entire project in which the progressives are involved.

If I am to be consistent with what I have said earlier in this book, I must judge this traditionalist reponse to be defective. There may be elements in contemporary thought and experience which, if incorporated in the Christian tradition as interpreted today, would enable it to reflect more completely the eternal truths which it is obliged to safeguard. It cannot be presumed in advance that the formulations of Christian ethics which have been accepted in the recent past are in no need of revision. They may need, as *Personal Origins* put it, to be 'extended and rethought'. On the other hand the whole tenor of my argument assumes that there must be limits to this process of revision. The fear on the part of traditionalists that the Church, or large parts of it, could lose its hold on Christian truth and forfeit in the process its Christian identity, is entirely warranted. We have in this country a local example in what happened to the Student Christian Movement in the 1960s and 1970s. Through its unwillingness to stand for anything distinctively Christian, it became almost entirely dissolved in the ambient secular atmosphere.

But, if there are to be limits, where are they to be found?

The first line to be held is that between regarding morality as a human construction only and seeing it, in Mackie's phrase, as 'required by the universe', or in more specifically Christian terms as the will of God. Hence, it is not invented, but discovered or revealed. To transgress the moral law is not just to breach the conventions of society or betray the norms which one has adopted for the conduct of one's life, but to violate principles in terms of which both of these may be judged, a violation which calls for repentance. Moral discernment is a human endowment, but one which needs divine grace to perfect it.

The autonomy of the will as conceived by Kant, developed by the Romantics and made almost the sole principle of morality by Nietzsche and his successors is an element of modern thought which cannot be assimilated into the Christian tradition. But it may, nevertheless, provide the impetus for a more sensitive understanding of the relationship in moral choice between grace and freedom. To acknowledge and to do God's will our own energies need to be fully exerted.

More specifically, there is a line which divides two distinctive attitudes to human life and human behaviour. One of them involves taking a section, as it were, of the individual's life at a particular moment and judging its value in terms of the characteristics it actually manifests at that time. It is on this basis that Helga Kuhse and Peter Singer assert that a mature pig is worthy of greater respect, as being more intelligent, socially aware, etc., than a mentally retarded man or a human baby.[11] The

---

[11] *Should the Baby Live?*, 122.

other regards human life as a continuum in which the individual remains a human subject throughout all the vicissitudes that may attend it, a conception that is memorably conveyed in the Prayer Book marriage service: 'for better or for worse, in sickness and in health, for richer for poorer, to love and to cherish until death do us part.'

This latter conception is not without its problems, but it is important to recognize that they arise at all only if the underlying notion of continuity is taken for granted: problems such as that of when human life actually starts or when it comes to an end. The moral acceptability of certain sorts of biological research turns on the answer to such questions, which is why they have been so hotly debated. But no such debate is necessary on the alternative view, because on that view it is only some time after birth that the child achieves rationality and the individual will often lose it before death. It is above all the experience of love which persuades us that people cannot be identified simply with the characteristics which they manifest at particular times. When we are deeply attached to a person, we cannot think of him or her in this way. What we love is a human being whose identity is continuous through life; and, moreover, one which is nourished at every stage by relationships with parents, friends, wives, and husbands, without which it would not fully develop. There is, moreover, something mysterious and inexhaustible about human beings which forbids us to value them simply and solely on account of those of their characteristics which we can fully understand and assess. It is not, then, surprising that A. S. Byatt's character, who had learnt to think of himself as 'a crossing place for a number of systems all loosely connected' had difficulty in falling in love. The progressive emphasis on the quality of life is evidently in danger of lapsing into the sort of secular attitude to life which the Christian tradition is bound to oppose. But there is a danger on the other side too: the traditional attitude to matters of life and death is itself liable to become divorced from any deep understanding of what human life is for and why God values it, so that its preservation in all circumstances becomes a bare matter of divine *fiat*.

There is a further line, more difficult to draw but needing to be drawn nevertheless, between behaviour which human beings are free to vary to suit their wishes and behaviour which is proper to human beings as such and is not, therefore, similarly variable. The issues treated by the Warnock Report lie on this boundary. To a large extent, they turned upon the nature of the marriage relationship and the extent to which the elements of procreation, mutual consolation and complementarity are essential to it. Nothing typifies the modern rejection of traditional Christian ethics more strikingly than the sexual revolution which came to a head in Europe and America in the 1960s. It became widely accepted that sexual activity should be enjoyed without restriction in all its manifestations; that to endeavour to limit it to marriage was both impracticable and unreasonable, and that the only constraints upon it should be those required to prevent exploitation.

The sexual revolution drew much of its force from a reaction against the Victorian and Edwardian practice of marriage with its subordination of women, its strong association of marriage with property and the hypocrisy and double standards for men and women which so often attended it. Most of this was not even at the time defended as Christian, but much of it was at least acquiesced in by the churches as representing an acceptable accommodation to the secular culture of the day.

There could be no question, then, of trying to hold the traditional line in the form it had assumed at that period, and liberal theologians and Christian ethicists have in the present century acceded to a generous impulse towards freedom and fairness in sexual relationships. Even progressives are not prepared, however, to go all the way with the sexual revolution and the criterion they propose to distinguish between what is and is not acceptable is that of love. Sexual intercourse is, and ought only to be, the expression of love between two persons, and, so long as this requirement is satisfied, no other constraints are needed. Here, then, is a clear case in which 'our traditions of moral thought need to be extended and rethought'.

Embedded in the traditional idea of marriage is the notion that sexual intercourse has its proper place in a relationship which is exclusive and permanent because it is designed for the procreation and education of children by partners who are complementary to one another both physically and psychologically. The relationship is such that the different elements in it reinforce one another. Mutual fidelity contributes to the security of the children, which in turn stengthens the bond between the parents, and helps the pair to grow as persons through the complete trust that they enjoy in one another. It is this interweaving of strands which shapes the institution of marriage, even if in a particular marriage there are no children. The progressive moralist's proposal to detach the 'unitive' end of marriage entirely from the 'procreative' leaves it unclear why a loving sexual relationship should be in intention permanent; and is in constant danger of sliding into the prevailing secular position.

I have insisted that this conception of marriage is not a merely conservative one, although it allows more to the traditionalists than many would like. Progressives ought not to abandon it, as many have, but rather ought to address themselves to the question, how best it can be accommodated to the conditions of the present time; how the institution of marriage itself requires to be modified; and how the ideal it represents can best be realized or approximated to, in cases where it cannot straightforwardly be achieved.

There is, I suggest, a way of reconciling traditionalist and progressive emphases in relation to these contentious matters. It is a way that is, in a sense, highly traditional—at least it derives from one long and coherent tradition, that of Catholic moral theology. The trouble with this tradition is that it has often been allowed to ossify in a manner quite alien to its origins in Aristotle and Aquinas, particularly in the debate about contraception. But it contains the resources which enable it continually to be 'extended and rethought'. By reflection on human nature as found in actual experience and as illuminated by the Christian tradition, it acknowledges principles of wide generality which have divine authority and are not merely human constructions. They are,

broadly speaking, the moral absolutes to which traditionalists appeal, but their interpretation requires us to
take account of whatever new sources of knowledge are
shown to be relevant, and their application to individual
cases demands awareness of and consideration for the
needs of persons in the particular situation in which they
find themselves. The result is inevitably somewhat
messy at times. It may upset traditionalists who can only
see what they regard as unwarranted exceptions being
made to clear-cut moral absolutes; they share the
reaction voiced by Mrs Kirk, in a remark which may or
may not be apocryphal, when asked her opinion of her
husband's work: 'Kenneth spends a great deal of his
time thinking of various subtle and sophisticated
reasons for doing things we all of us know to be
wrong.'[12] At the same time, it often outrages the
progressives who see careful discriminations being
made, and cautious concessions allowed when what is
being demanded are basic human rights.

How the 'extending and rethinking of our moral
thought' goes on is well put by Oliver O'Donovan:

We learn more about the moral law as we think about
difficult cases ... We penetrate behind the straightforward-
ness of the moral code through which we first learnt the
moral law to discover that that law is as complex and
pluriform as the created order itself which it reflects.

And if we fail to learn in this way? If we cling to the
simplicity of the code as we first knew it? In that case the
pressure of new experience which historical contingency

---

[12] The reference is to the great Anglican moral theologian, Kenneth
Kirk (1886–1954).

forces upon us will soon bring us to the breaking point. We shall recognize suddenly that the categories of our moral understanding are no longer sufficient to interpret our situation and we shall rebel wildly and disorderedly against them.[13]

It is in this way that in morality, tradition and criticism inform and reinforce each other.

[13] *Resurrection and the Moral Order* (Leicester: Inter-Varsity Press, 1986), 195.

7

Religious Education

The problem of faith and criticism arises where there are rival systems of thought between which the individual has to choose, or behave as if he had chosen. Adherence to one of these, whether it is religious or not, requires the capacity to maintain one's convictions and resist temptation to abandon them prematurely or modify them without due reason. But it is also necessary to recognize the force of criticisms and take them into account in the formulation of one's convictions. This applies equally to corporate bodies, with the rider that the two functions of safeguarding the faith and submitting it to criticism are often entrusted to groups of people who by temperament or training are suited to the one task or the other.

This situation poses a problem for educators. What account, if any, shall they take of the need for individuals to find a faith to live by and of society to pass on its inherited beliefs and values together with the capacity to reflect intelligently about them? There would seem to be three possible policies:

One is to keep clear of world-views altogether, to limit education to academic and vocational subjects and to adopt a purely pragmatic policy when moral decisions have inescapably to be made.

The second is to deal with them explicitly, but from an entirely neutral or 'phenomenological' standpoint. One should not teach Christianity or any other religion or philosophy of life, but rather teach about them.

The third is to 'induct' the young into one of them (or more than one in so far as they are compatible) while taking care to be fair to others.

In this country, for historical reasons connected with the fact of Establishment and the Church's pioneering work in education, the first option has never been seriously considered. It has, in any case, the severe drawback that, if educators refrain from exercising a definite influence upon the young, the result will be not that they remain free from bias, but that other agencies will impart it. One of these agencies, the family, has, in any case, a crucial role to play, but it is one which many families, in the circumstances of modern life, find hard to play without assistance.

The second option has received strong support among educationalists for much of the post-war period and remains influential less as an explicit policy than as a ghost which haunts discussion of any other alternative. This is because fairness is required by any acceptable policy, and this one is the most straightforwardly fair.

Or so it might seem. The trouble is that in practice, inevitably, the desired neutrality is not uniformly distributed. The educators themselves, and the school or college as an institution, cannot take a purely 'phenomenological' line about some matters. I was vividly reminded of this when visiting an American university and enjoying the generous hospitality which is so readily extended to strangers. A group of faculty members were talking together after dinner and the conversation turned to the subject of plagiarism, which was apparently on the increase on that campus. Students were including in the course papers which were to be graded chunks of material from books and articles without acknowledgement. The majority of those present were rather reluctantly persuaded that this practice ought to be explicitly forbidden, but a sizeable minority were very uneasy about this. Their view was that the offenders, if such they were, represented an alternative ethic, widely prevalent among the student body, which maintained that the point of going to college was to get a degree and the point of a degree was to get a job, and no blame should be attached to someone who simply took prudent measures to guarantee success. Who were they, as faculty members, to impose upon their students their own traditional moral standards?

They had, by the end of the evening, regretfully concluded that, if they wanted to remain members of an academic community, they had to take a line on cheating. Any school will, similarly, need to outlaw stealing, bullying, truancy, not to mention drug dealing and other criminal offences.

Up to a point, the authorities can plausibly maintain that these prohibitions are only pragmatic. There are certain things that the pupils may not do because the existence or reputation of the school will suffer if they do. They must observe the law and they must take some account of public opinion. But to advance this claim in all such cases would be disingenuous. The prohibitions are enforced because the behaviour prohibited is held to be wrong and it is part of the school's job to show concern for the moral development of pupils. To the extent that this is so, it cannot be content with a purely phenomenological approach: 'there are some people who believe that it is wrong to cheat; others, however, believe it to be justified.' Moreover, any school worth its salt will rather risk public disfavour than compromise standards to which it is committed. Racial discrimination may be rife in the neighbourhood and part of the culture of the area, but the school will feel bound to stand against it, no matter how unpopular this may make it. An article in *The Times* based on educational research done at Manchester University said: ' "Boys and girls still see themselves as . . . each with their own role to play. Most of them believe that boys repair cars while girls wash clothes." What should the teacher do? 83.8% said they tried to counteract such stereotyping.' The article went on to ask, 'Are they wise? Who are they to go against the family and other social pressures? What is their mandate?' These questions may be variously answered, but they cannot be evaded. The school must take some line on what gender roles are appropriate and will not, as a rule, regard itself as bound automatically by attitudes at present prevalent in society. Society too has to be educated and the place to start is the school.

Another equally controversial example is that of sex education. If the school is a boarding school, rules will be needed governing sexual behaviour and may range from the full acceptance of temporary partnerships at the experimental school at Summerhill to the 'no-touching' regime of some more traditional independent schools. There is, of course, a strong pragmatic element in the decisions made. The resolutely progressive parents of the Summerhill children apart, most parents do not want their offspring to be encouraged to engage in sexual intercourse, as it would seem to them, prematurely, even though surveys suggest that many of them will. Nevertheless, it is reasonable to presume that behind the policy lies a conviction, on the part of the school authorities themselves, that their charges are not yet ready to enter into a responsible relationship.

Apart from these practical arrangements, where they are needed, there is increasing pressure upon schools to provide explicit sex education, which will prepare the young for the decisions they will have to make. The threat of AIDS intensifies the need. There is widespread agreement that instruction about sex should be given in the context of advice about personal relationships in general, sometimes as part of 'Personal and Social Education'. But in practice this is difficult and, one suspects, often evaded. The simplest and most straight-forward policy is to be severely practical and concentrate upon the overriding importance of avoiding pregnancy and contact with the HIV virus. The use of condoms will be explained and condoms themselves perhaps distributed. The alarming incidence of teenage pregnancies (together with the threat of AIDS) is thought to render any other approach impossible.

Although the intention is to avoid 'moralizing', the policy itself embodies clear moral assumptions which will not escape the notice of those to whom it is addressed. It implies that, if there are moral constraints upon sexual activity, they are of comparatively little

importance and are liable to be ineffective. This implication will remain even if attention is paid to the ethics of
personal relations. If these are treated in a phenomenological way and the young are told that 'some people
believe' that, for example, sexual intercourse should be
the expression of a loving relationship which is in
intention permanent, the belief will have virtually no
authority besides the pragmatic message which says:
'You will, of course, be sexually active and there is
nothing wrong with this so long as you take adequate
precautions.' And if the school lends its authority to the
kind of moral teaching which could counteract the
effects that the pragmatic approach would have on its
own, the task of relating the two in a coherent fashion
will not be easy. Nevertheless, it needs to be undertaken.
Educators cannot, in practice, avoid taking a moral
stance even if they try to be purely pragmatic or resolve
to treat alternative moralities in a spirit of complete
neutrality.

Given the extent to which the positions people adopt
in relation to personal and social ethics are systematically
bound up with their whole philosophy of life, whether
religious or secular, it becomes evident that it is not
possible to seek neutrality about these either. In fact, as
we have seen, educators do not hesitate, as a rule, to
communicate convictions to which they are really
committed, even when they are not shared by society at
large. They see it as part of their larger educational role
to contribute, in so far as they can, to altering the
attitudes of society, beginning in the schools.

It follows that religious education as a requirement
in schools needs no defence against the charge of

indoctrination which is still frequently brought against it, in so far as it represents the handing on of a received tradition from one generation to another. It is, of course, open to attack on the part of those who would rather that some other and incompatible tradition of thought were handed on, and that is a legitimate subject for political debate; but it is entirely disingenuous to promote a particular alternative point of view in the guise of observing neutrality.

Let us anchor the discussion in the religious education provisions of the 1988 Education Reform Act, because the concerns of educationalists about Christian education have been voiced recently in relation to the Act. The author of *The Times*' article quoted earlier, commenting on the expressed willingness of teachers to take a line on gender roles, asked, 'What is their mandate?' The mandate for religious education in schools is to be found in the Act as are the requirements that agreed syllabuses 'shall reflect the fact that the religious traditions in Great Britian are in the main Christian' and that school worship 'shall be wholly or mainly of a broad Christian character'. In addition, the Circular on Religious Education and Worship states that 'all those concerned with religious education should seek to ensure that it promotes respect, understanding and tolerance for those of other faiths'. The evidence of opinion polls is that these provisions have wide public support.

Critics of the Act are for the most part exercised by the old fear of indoctrination and by the thought that the predominance accorded to Christianity will be 'divisive' and will consign adherents of other religions to an inferior status.

I have stated boldly that the charge of indoctrination must fail if it is accepted that education cannot be neutral about beliefs and values, but this judgement needs qualifying. The fear of indoctrination, although not justified in relation to religious education as such, is appropriate to certain ways in which it may be conducted. I have argued elsewhere,[1] and still maintain, that the charge of indoctrination applies to the use of methods in teaching religion or anything else, which are intended to produce, or do in fact produce, closed minds and restricted sympathies. Blanket condemnation of religious education reflects the belief that it cannot avoid doing this. The underlying assumption is simply the one we have discussed and rejected, viz. that religious faith, especially and specifically, Christian faith, is whole-hearted and unconditional and therefore cannot allow of criticism. It would follow that it could not be fair and impartial in its treatment of other faiths or philosophies of life. If that were so, the project of inducting people into a religious tradition of this kind would be contrary to the principles of any sort of liberal education.

That Christian teaching has often proceeded in this way and still sometimes does cannot be denied. The same is true of the way other faiths are often taught and not only religious faiths. Marxism was systematically inculcated for most of this century in just this way and a vigorous censorship of opposing views is not unknown in circles where progressive attitudes are dominant.

But the entire onus of this book has been to insist that

[1] See *The Fourth R: The Durham Report on Religious Education* (London: SPCK, 1970), 353–8.

there is no incompatibility between whole-hearted faith and openness to criticism. For any developed tradition to maintain itself in a healthy state, faith and criticism must reinforce one another. Hence, to be religiously educated is not a matter of being led to accept in an uncritical and unreflective way, a set of beliefs and values, which are themselves so neatly parcelled that they can properly be handed over in this way, but of being encouraged to share in a tradition which is continuously being rethought and reapplied. This is not incompatible with the requirement that tolerance and understanding be shown to those of other faiths, but is rather a precondition of it. No-one can even begin to understand and evaluate profound and complex systems of religious belief without having been inducted initially into some one religious tradition.

The more temperate critics of specifically Christian religious education tend no longer to rely on the charge of indoctrination, but to express their concern instead in terms of a distinction between 'education' and 'nurture'. Religious education must, they insist, be treated in schools in such a way as to be genuinely educational and this approach must be carefully distinguished from Christian nurture. Hence, some commentators upon the 1988 legislation have welcomed the emphasis in it on teaching Christianity as a dominant influence upon English culture, an emphasis which, they believe, allows them to maintain a purely phenomenological approach and avoid questions of truth and falsehood.

But it is far from clear that, in general terms, there is any firm distinction between education and nurture, or that the latter is ruled out in the Act, or by the regular practice of schools in this country. The White Paper speaks of physical, mental and spiritual development and the encouragement of this is what 'nurture' normally means. And this is made more explicit in the White Paper's declaration that 'at the heart of a school's educational and pastoral policy and practice should lie a set of shared values promoted through the curriculum and expectations governing behaviour of pupils and staff'.[2]

Leaving religious education aside, it is impossible to teach history or literature without assuming and imparting a sense of what is or is not vicious or virtuous, worthwhile or of little value. The process involves encouraging increasingly the individual's capacity for creative imagination and independent criticism, but it is folly to suppose that one can learn to be critical and creative without first having been introduced to something of substance capable of seizing the imagination and stimulating criticism. The point is entirely general. The way to help people become genuinely creative and critical is not to try to bring them up without imparting to them any definite beliefs and values but to offer them a coherent framework—the best one is able to find—within which they can grow, or, if they choose, eventually reject with some understanding of what they are doing. Unending debates in educational circles about whether the teaching of history should seek to develop skills or communicate knowledge provide a textbook example of the dangers of posing false alternatives.

The attempt to distinguish between education and

---

[2] *The Times*, 29 July 1992.

nurture is not, therefore, as helpful as it might at first have seemed. Yet, clearly, there is an important distinction to be made which this terminology is attempting to mark. In a preliminary way, it can be approached by distinguishing between what is proper in the classroom and what is proper in a church. The sort of 'nurture' that is inappropriate is nurture in a specific religious or denominational tradition. Where state or county schools are concerned, in which different denominations are represented and some of those present belong to other faiths or to no faith at all, it would indeed be inappropriate for teaching to be given which is peculiar to a single denomination, for example, about Church order, or about the sacraments. Such teaching would not, however, be out of place in an Anglican or Roman Catholic-aided school or in an independent school with a religious foundation. This would not be because it involved nurture rather than education but because the nurture/education given was inappropriate to its context.

If there is something which would be acceptable in church, but not in the classroom, one would expect to recognize the distinction as applying across the board, no matter what the type of school—as much in a denominational school as in a non-denominational one. As a first approximation one might suggest that it is proper in church, but not in the classroom, to presume commitment on the part of the individual. Of course, not all of those present in church may in fact be committed, but what takes place assumes that they are and rightly so. In the classroom, on the other hand, where criticism is accepted and even encouraged, there is no such assumption.

This will not quite do. For, as I have been arguing all along, commitment and criticism do not mutually exclude one another. Even if it could be presumed that the students in the classroom were committed, there would still be a necessary place for criticism there. So it is not the presence or absence of commitment that is crucial, but the presence or absence of criticism. In the classroom, criticism is always in place (although needless to say, not always at every point. There is much that at any given time must be taken on authority.). In worship in church, though, there is need for some analogue of 'that willing suspension of disbelief for the moment' which, according to Coleridge, 'constitutes poetic faith'. (Whether this applies to the sermon I have never quite been able to decide.)

At an earlier stage in this book I compared religious faith to trust between persons[3] and argued that our capacity to love someone, and the character of that love, cannot be dissociated from the way in which we conceive the nature of human beings. And I claimed that the fact that we are committed whole-heartedly to people when we love them does not imply that the concepts we employ in our understanding and assessment of persons are beyond revision. There is thus an essential place for critical thought in our relationship with persons. It does not follow in the least that critical thought is appropriate in all phases of our intercourse with people and there are times when it is most certainly out of place. Indeed it would be fair to say that its role, although indispensable, is subordinate.

[3] See Ch. 2, pp. 41 f.; Ch. 4, pp. 83 ff.

In worship, then, criticism is suspended—and rightly so. It must not, however, be suspended in the classroom. There are other constraints which should operate in the classroom where children are concerned and which some may think need not operate in worship. Children, particularly in adolescence, require a personal space, within which they are free to be themselves or decide who they are or want to be. They should not, then, be subjected to undue emotional or intellectual pressure. Any commitments they may make at this stage have to be regarded as to some extent provisional and not to be presumed upon excessively. Teachers are, for the most part, well aware that they should not use their authority and the strength of their personalities to impose upon their pupils beliefs and attitudes to life in such a way that they may not later be able to modify or abandon them even if they find good reason to do so. Which is another way of saying that they should avoid indoctrination.

It seems to follow that a certain restraint should be observed in forms of worship as well. Although criticism is suspended, the individual's freedom should not be compromised by invasive methods of psychological manipulation. There is a line to be drawn between a free response to experiences which are deeply moving and a yielding to emotional pressure. But can worship be free if it is undertaken as a corporate act required by law? Many people who accept the case for religious education of a predominantly Christian character and who agree that it cannot be neutral, nevertheless reject the requirement of Christian worship. Some argue that it is a 'contradiction in terms' from which it follows that it should not be attempted in schools of any kind, including those with a Christian foundation. Others object to it only in state schools, where it cannot be presumed that the pupils or their parents are believers and where there may be representatives of other faiths.

To some extent it is the corporate nature of the worship which excites suspicion. It is felt that worship is essentially an individual activity and that it should take place only by the free association of individuals. It is for this reason, perhaps, that the expression 'collective worship' is used in the legislation rather than 'corporate' worship. But there are in the life of all communities occasions when there is a spontaneous wish to come together as a community to celebrate some great event or seek strength and consolation in some tragedy or pray for someone in desperate need. It is appropriate to do these things and they are done in the name of the institution and not simply of the individuals who constitute it. No doubt many of those who take part are only fitfully or not at all religious, but they wish to associate themselves with the corporate act. In later life they will from time to time find themselves in this situation.

School worship is not only a corporate or collective act. It is an opportunity for those who take part in it to learn what worship is and to understand better what is meant by the religious language which they are required to study. They cannot be expected to develop empathy with Christian thought and feeling if they have no experience of it from the inside; nor can they show due respect for the worship of other faiths if they have no direct acquaintance with worship of any kind themselves. So far as individuals are concerned, the object must be to enable them, as far as possible, to decide when they reach maturity, what convictions are to govern their lives. They cannot decide for or against Christianity unless they have become acquainted with it from within, and that implies being given the opportunity to worship. The notion of moral and spiritual development presupposes this, since, though it has an intellectual component, it cannot be purely intellectual. This means that some bias is imparted by the educational process in favour of a Christian formation which might have been directed elsewhere—towards a wholly secular outlook, for example. What is not an option is the avoidance of bias altogether. The bias would be objectionable if it left the adult psychologically crippled, intellectually impaired, or spiritually insensitive, and care must be taken to prevent this happening.

The inclusion of worship in a programme of religious education involves, in effect, a sort of guided devotional experiment, designed to enable those who take part in it to taste and see for themselves a spiritual reality which is not as a rule immediately apparent, but which, if it exists at all, is of supreme importance. Any such experiment does, of course, presuppose that there is good reason to believe in the reality which is being sought. Such a presupposition may reasonably be entertained in schools which are run by religious bodies or have an explicitly religious foundation. But it may be objected that it is totally out of place in the state educational system of a secular, plural, and multicultural society. In the next chaper I want to examine the claim that our own society is properly so described.

So far in this chapter I have argued that, given the interdependence of faith and criticism, religious education can and should be both committed and critical. It is best thought of not as attempting to transmit a completed body of knowledge, but as introducing the young into a living tradition in which a process of trusting and testing is going on all the time. But it has to be admitted that the task of religious education, so understood, is severely hampered by features of the cultural situation in which the educators have to operate. Prominent among these is the tendency to regard science as the only avenue to truth, and to conceive science itself in a narrowly restrictive way. Hence, everything that is not science is thought of dismissively as poetry, expressive of private emotion, and immune from rational criticism. There is evidence that this kind of naive scientism affects children at quite an early age with the result that religious faith has either to emulate science (as science is thought to be) by treating its claims also in a flat literalistic way, or accept the status of an entirely subjective response to the world as known through science. Moreover, any attempt to ground religious belief in a coherent tradition of thought runs into the difficulty people today have in placing themselves consciously in a historical tradition of any sort.

It follows that a programme of religious education cannot be satisfactorily pursued in isolation from the rest of the curriculum. Science teaching requires to do justice to the nature of scientific explanation, the role of imagination in scientific discovery, and the place of models and metaphors in scientific thinking. There is available, in fact, very good material for use in schools which draws intelligently upon recent work in the history and philosophy of science. Children need some understanding of the resemblances and differences between the way language is used in the sciences and the humanities if they are to develop any feeling for typical uses of religious language, and it is not to be expected that they will get far with that unless they are encouraged to become familiar with some of the classics of Christian literature. Religious education suffers if pupils lack a sense of history or a feeling for language.

At this point there is in fact a convergence between two purposes of religious education which are often thought to be in conflict: the need to transmit a national and a European culture which has been deeply influenced by Christianity, and the aim of developing a genuine understanding of Christianity itself. It is often thought by sincere advocates of the latter aim that to the extent that one is impressed by the splendour of language, music, architecture, and the other arts as expressive of the Christian faith, one is being seduced from the true Gospel—for these things are mere embellishments. But, whatever may have been true in the past, when a move to simplify and purify the tradition was a needed contribution to it, the tradition itself being taken for granted, the result of such a posture now is all too often sheer impoverishment.

One of the most successful ways of helping children to enter into the living tradition of other faiths has been to observe or take part in their festivals or regular rituals which, apart from developing insight into these faiths, can also revive or intensify interest in the significance of ritual in the Christian tradition. The point is well put by the present Archbishop of York:

A religiously educated person needs a sense of the way in which social life depends on ritual but is not circumscribed by ritual; a sense of the importance of ritual in maintaining social systems, of the importance of non-verbal ways of expressing meanings. We are all creatures of ritual, whether we like it or not. Ritual can, of course, become empty; but without rituals we are to a large extent socially lost, as we can be religiously lost.

One observes this sometimes at a wedding or a funeral when people have deep emotions to express but have lost or never been taught any accepted way of expressing them.

It is less easy than it used to be to discern a moral consensus in this country. This is bound to make moral education both more difficult and more necessary. There are some who would wish to keep religion out of moral education altogether, but whichever end one starts from—the religious or the moral—it is hard to see how this can be done. No religious education can be adequate which leaves the moral implications of religious faith unexplored and if the education is to be predominantly Christian, this requires a study of Christian ethics. No moral education is complete if it neglects the fundamental questions about the nature and purpose of human life which largely shape our moral convictions.

Where moral issues are the subject of controversy, their controversial nature cannot and should not be disguised. In sixth forms, discussion of them inspires lively interest and leads rapidly into quite deep questions of philosophy and theology.

I have been arguing in this book that it is possible and necessary to be fair to opposing points of view while holding to firm convictions of one's own and letting these convictions be known; and this applies to institutions as well as to individuals. So a church-related school or an independent school with a religious foundation need not hesitate to adhere to Christian principles in its religious teaching and, indeed, in the entire ethos of the school. It will not necessarily be different in a state school; but in any school, whatever its status, it is evident that account must be taken of the background and outlook of those who learn and teach in it. This is obvious, so far as the pupils are concerned, when as sometimes happens many, perhaps a majority of them, belong to other faiths, but it applies equally where many of the staff have no Christian affiliations. They cannot be expected to express opinions which they do not hold or take part in ceremonies to which they conscientiously object, but they are not, I think, entitled to regard the requirements of the law, which have firm public support, as of no importance. They do have a responsibility, as members of a corporate body, to consider how the school can best make provision for the spiritual as well as the intellectual and physical development of their charges.

We have seen that, in whatever types of school, religious teaching and religious worship, except when entirely voluntary, are not designed to secure commitment as their immediate aim but to ensure that the young are given the resources for making a decision in their own time and for continuing to grow in understanding when the decision has been made. This means that a contribution can be made by teachers who are not themselves believers so long as they are willing and able to take Christianity seriously and enter into it imaginatively, even when making it clear that they do not personally accept it.

No treatment of religion can be satisfactory which does not make clear that eventually commitment is involved, but so far as the educational process itself is concerned, there is much wisdom in a passage in the writings of H. H. Price. It occurs towards the end of his monumental Gifford Lectures on *Belief*: he is talking about the Gospel narratives.

The important thing is not that we should believe these narratives, or how firmly we believe them, if we do. What is recommended is that we should think of them assiduously and attentively, think over them and ruminate upon them . . . We may also believe these [religious] propositions or some of them, but the important thing is that we should be *interested* in them, interested enough to try to realize fully what their content is and to let our thoughts dwell on them. If we believe them without being interested in them, and without any tendency at all to ruminate over them or meditate upon them, we cannot expect that this will have much effect in developing spiritual capacities. What we think about privately and inwardly, and think about often, is much more important from this point of view than what we believe, and much more likely to alter our personalities. Belief can come later.[4]

[4] (London: George Allen & Unwin, 1969), 478.

8

The Perils of 'Pluralism'

In the United States the constitutional separation of church and state—'Congress shall make no law respecting an establishment of religion'—ensures that there is a lively and continuous debate about the place of religion in public life: to what extent does the Constitution allow religious considerations to influence policy? In England there is no such debate. To be sure, the existence of an established Church might seem to render such debate unnecessary. Establishment must mean that the Church has the duty and the privilege of tendering advice on matters affecting the moral and spiritual well-being of the nation. Although in a democratic society it has no prescriptive right to determine policy, it may reasonably expect its advice to be attended to. Like the monarch's, its role is 'to be consulted, to advise, and to warn'. In an ecumenical age it is arguable that this role should be shared by other Christian churches, but establishment in any form presupposes that the Christian religion has an acknowledged position in the country.

Many, probably a majority of people in the country, understand the position in this way, but a sizeable minority, especially among the intelligentsia, take a different view. They regard this country as being already, in effect, a secular state or a 'plural society' on the American model, lacking only explicit constitutional recognition. The legal establishment of the Church of England they take to be an historical anomaly which can safely be disregarded in practice. How, they are inclined to ask, can a small minority of practising Anglicans have any status on a national scale? How, indeed, could the religious preferences of the few (or even of the many) possess significance outside the purely private sphere in which they properly belong? The notion that Christian beliefs and values should have any recognition in public life is repudiated, not, overtly at least, in order that some other set of values should take their place, but because it is assumed that, as a society, we need no common values over and above the minimum necessary to hold society together. The expression 'in our plural society' is generally used to represent this point of view. The assumption is that the Church of England will tacitly accept the purely private role that is offered it and will be content to regard the establishment as a dead letter. Hence the consternation in parts of the educational world when the then Bishop of London succeeded in amending the Education Act to ensure that acts of worship in state schools should be predominantly Christian—a provision that might be thought non-controversial in a country with an established church.

If we wish to address the question of how far Christian values should be reflected in the public policy of a country like ours, it looks as if we need to decide whether ours is, in any sense, a Christian society, or whether it is, by contrast, a plural or multicultural society. If ours is a Christian society, then, it might be thought, Christian values should prevail as of right. If ours is a plural/multicultural society, then no set of substantive moral values should prevail in it; there should be no conception of a common good. These questions, however, are far from easy to answer. There are certain features which suggest that ours is a Christian country:

(*a*) We have an established Church. There is no formal separation of church and state, as there is in the USA.

(*b*) 88 per cent of the population profess themselves Christian.[1]

(*c*) Christianity has been, without any doubt, the greatest single influence upon our national culture.

Nevertheless, it is also the case that:

(*a*) there is a comparatively low proportion of active churchgoers—10 per cent according to the latest Church census.

(*b*) there are sizeable minorities of non-Christians, of whom a much larger proportion than among professing Christians are active adherents of their own religions.

Perhaps, in the light of these facts, the verdict of the MORI volume itself is the best we can manage:

But can Britain be called a Christian nation? One thing at least we can clear up right away. It certainly isn't anything else. There is much talk of Britain having become a multi-faith society. But our survey threw up little evidence of this.

[1] Eric Jacobs and Robert Worcester, *We British: Britain under the Moriscope* (London: Weidenfeld and Nicolson, 1990), 77–8. Other surveys yield somewhat different figures, but the variations are not large enough to affect the main argument.

Only about 1 per cent of our respondents was Jewish and
another 1 per cent Moslem. Other non-Christian faiths
registered only a further 1 per cent between them. When we
talk about how religious the British might be we still
overwhelmingly mean, how Christian?

The answer to that question, we discovered, varies
according to what we mean by it. If we mean, do people wish
to be identified with one or another denomination of the
Christian Church, then the answer is an overwhelming 'yes'.
If we mean, do they subscribe to the central beliefs of the
Christian faith, then the answer will be much less confident,
but it will still be a hesitant 'yes'.

But if we mean, do they follow through their identification
with a Church and their attachment to Christian beliefs by
regular or frequent church-going, then the answer must be an
emphatic 'no'.

However, the answers provided by the MORI survey do
not go very far towards helping us deal with the central
problem. We need to have a clearer notion of what is
meant by talk of a Christian country or a plural or
multi-cultural society. When people deny that Britian is
a Christian country, what state of affairs would have to
obtain for that description, in their view, to be applicable? Something like the following:

(*a*) A high proportion of the population would have
to be regular churchgoers—at least as high as the 40 per
cent registered in the United States;

(*b*) An even higher proportion would have to believe
in the central doctrines of Christianity, say, in God, in
the divinity of Christ, and eternal life;

(*c*) It should be formally accepted, and informally
conceded that, wherever in matters of personal or social
ethics there exists a distinctively Christian point of view,

this should automatically be reflected in legislation and social policy.

The actual situation in this country is far from satisfying the description, which would, indeed, apply at all fully only to such countries as Ireland and Franco's Spain (in which pre-Vatican II doctrines of the relation between church and state prevailed). But failure to achieve this inappropriate standard should not be taken as deciding the issue of the influence of Christianity in Britain (or, more specifically, England).

In trying to estimate the extent of the influence of the Christian churches in this country one has to decide how to relate the evidence about churchgoing and other 'churchy' activities to the information derived from opinion polls, television and radio programme ratings, and other social surveys. When statistics about church attendance alone are taken as the clue, it is the Church of England which suffers the greatest distortion of its actual level of support. Roman Catholics and Muslims are able to retain as regular worshippers a very much higher proportion of their nominal adherents than the Church of England can, as is likely to be the case with minority groups. Any estimate of the influence of the Church of England must largely depend on what view is taken of the immense penumbra of uncommitted Anglicans.

A preliminary protest must be entered at the journalistic habit of concentrating attention upon the number of active churchgoers. Some corrective to this is provided by the parallel case of political parties. An article in *The Times* on 23 September 1991 says of the two main political parties: 'Membership figures are highly unreliable, but all parties have suffered a substantial decline over the past 15 to 20 years. The Tory total fell from 2.8 million in the early 1950s to just under 1.2 million by the early 1980s, and is probably even lower now. Labour's total individual membership was more than a million in the early 1950s but has since fallen sharply.'[2] Comparison with figures for church attendance is obviously problematic but, judged by this standard, the much talked of 'decline of the churches' takes on a different complexion. If the strength of the political parties was judged not simply by membership but by regular attendance at party meetings, the point would be even clearer.

The article goes on to say: 'the parties themselves blame social changes: people now have a wider range of choices about how to spend their time,' and in this they are right. There are all sorts of factors, such as greater mobility, the attractions of television and all the social processes which sociologists know as 'privatization', which have weakened both established social institutions and voluntary associations in the post-war period. If a comparative study were made, it might well be found that the churches have resisted erosion more effectively than most comparable institutions. It would be interesting to know what the response of the Chairman of the Conservative Party would be, if it were put to him that with a low and declining membership of less than two per cent of the population, the Tory Party, as representative of a tiny minority, had no claim to exercise a

[2] However, an article in *The Independent*, 13 Oct. 1993, gives a figure of 4000,000.

predominant influence upon public policy in this country.

But, as the MORI survey makes clear, there is a very much larger proportion of the population who acknowledge some relationship with a Christian church and who accept, although often incompletely and inaccurately, some version of the major Christian doctrines, who engage in prayer, who watch religious programmes on television, who attend church occasionally, or who lend their support financially or through voluntary labour to the preservation of church buildings or the work of Christian charities. Not to mention the role of the Church in the celebration of key moments in the life of the state and of individual families and also of innumerable intermediate institutions.

Those who would maintain that this country is, in every sense that matters, a secular society, have to dismiss all this as an anomalous survival into the modern world of vestiges of an older culture which can be safely discountd in any serious debate about the realities of contemporary life—although no secular substitute for them is available, and there is little indication that we can do without them. The secularist disparagement of 'the penumbra' is supported by many progressive Christian thinkers who tend to repudiate what they think of as 'folk religion' in the name of a more authentic Christian witness. They would gladly be rid of it and be set free to concentrate their energies upon the building up of truly Christian communities in conscious opposition to society at large.

However, we are not concerned with the question whether ours is a Christian society in any full-blooded sense; we have already agreed that it is not. The question is to what extent Christian beliefs and values continue to be influential in it. In relation to this three further points require to be made.

(*a*) Our earlier argument has emphasized the extent to which those who to some degree accept a system of religious belief vary as to the elements in it to which they give credence. Hence, the evidence of opinion polls indicates that fewer people believe in the divinity of Christ than do in God the Creator, and fewer still in a life to come. It would be fair to say, on this showing, that less than half the population gives assent to orthodox Christianity as traditionally understood.

(*b*) However, our earlier argument also leads us not to overrate the importance in people's lives of explicit and articulate thought. What matters (except for intellectuals who have a vocation to be articulate) is how they respond in practice and in imagination to the vicissitudes of life. The extent of Christian influence is not adequately measured by formal assent to doctrines.

(*c*) What has often puzzled observers in Britain (and, once again, more specifically, England) is the combination of widespread indifference to church-going or 'organized religion' with a prevailing standard of decent behaviour, which is sufficient to persuade most people that 'one doesn't have to go to church in order to be good'. It is often assumed, indeed, that those who go to church think themselves better than other people so that to refrain from church-going is a mark of Christian humility. Even now outside church circles to call someone 'a Christian' often means not that he is a believer, let alone a churchgoer, but rather that he is honest, fair and considerate of others. When Newman despaired of bringing the English to a dogmatic temper he failed to notice, or perhaps just was not impressed by, the extent to which they took it for granted that what mattered in religion was its effect upon conduct.

The conclusion must be that there is a lot of diffused Christianity around, non-dogmatic, moralistic, shown predominantly in attitudes towards people. The Church is viewed as a reliable source of this, to which all except a devoted (and somewhat suspect) few return only occasionally for the expression of public or private grief or the celebration of key moments in life. It is assumed that the Church will be there, and conspicuously there, and will continue to perform this function without the individual's having to do anything about it. People treat the Church much as adolescents do their parents. They have always been there and are useful in emergencies.

The MORI survey concluded that, if Britain was not a Christian country, it certainly was not anything else. In this it rejected the thesis which is commonly taken for granted that ours is a 'post-Christian' society, which is properly characterized as secular, pluralistic, multi-faith, multicultural. That some of all of these terms are applicable is frequently taken to provide the premise for wide-ranging arguments about the scope and character of legislation and social policy. It is, therefore, necessary, but also difficult, to be clear as to what they mean.

(a) A plural or multicultural society, in its most straightforward sense, is one in which minority groups are free to maintain their independent cultural traditions. This is the common dictionary definition. In this sense Britain is plainly a plural society, but nothing follows from it about how the wider society orders itself, so long as it gives this freedom to minorities.

(*b*) A plural society is one in which ethnic or religious minorities comprise a comparatively high proportion of the total population—sufficiently high to prevent one regarding any single group as predominant. Britain in this sense is not a plural or multicultural society, since, as the MORI report points out, the minority groups form a very small proportion of the total population. The term could, however, be applied to certain areas of the country where such minorities are concentrated. Although Britain is not a multicultural society in this sense, the presence of these minorities and their concentration in certain localities does raise serious questions about how they can be made to feel at home in the wider society.

(*c*) A plural society is one in which there is no recognition of shared values, no conception of a common good. This may simply be a *de facto* judgement based upon the comparatively heterogeneous character of the society in question (as would be the case where it is 'plural' in sense (b)); or it may be a theoretical judgement, to which members of the society are presumed to agree, to the effect that, even if there is agreement about a common good, it would be wrong to embody it in legislation or social policy. Although Britain is plainly not a plural society in the first of these senses, there are many thinkers of a liberal temper who hold that it is, or ought to be, a plural society in this theoretical sense. Indeed, it has been something of a platitude in social and legal theory to distinguish between a public morality which comprises only those principles which are needed to keep a society in being and a private morality which derives from the preferences of individuals and voluntary groups and applies only to them. But Britain is not, in this sense, a plural society; indeed such a society is impossible. Very few people, in fact, consistently uphold this ideal of pluralism. Those who claim to be doing so are, in effect, seeking to promote an alternative set of values in the larger society.

(*d*) There is a further sense of 'plural society' which requires to be mentioned because it is the cause of serious confusions. This is its use as a synonym for 'liberal society', that is to say, one in which fundamental human rights are respected, freedom of thought, expression, and association guaranteed, and legal protection afforded to minorities. When we are invited to welcome the advent of a new 'pluralism' to the countries of the former USSR and of Eastern Europe, what is meant is that they are on the way to becoming liberal democracies.

Given this variety of meanings, it is not surprising that there is a strong tendency to slide imperceptibly from one to another, and indeed it is part of a certain political rhetoric to encourage this slide. If we are prepared to agree, as most of us are, that Britian is, or at least aims to be, a liberal society, and that there are in it significant minorities whose interests and susceptibilities deserve consideration, and if we are persuaded to express this agreement in terms of the proposition that Britain is a plural or a multicultural society, we are then presumed to have accepted the dubious contention that Britain is or ought to be a plural society in a quite different sense. We find ourselves committed to a range of policies in the field of education, the family, even the use of language, which are not implied by anything we are in fact prepared to concede, but which can plausibly be said to follow from the terminology of 'pluralism' and 'multi-culturalism' which we have been led to employ.

How this works can readily be seen in the case of religious education. The fact that ours is a plural or multicultural society in the limited sense in which this is true, makes it a reasonable requirement that the young should be taught about the religions that are represented in this country in such a way as to encourage under-standing and toleration of them. It does not require that religious education should not be predominantly Christian. If, however, ours were a plural society in the sense of one which acknowledges no shared values, it would follow at once that no public recognition should be given to Christian (or any other) positive beliefs and values, and that they should not provide the basis for education. Either religious education should be omitted altogether from the curriculum in state schools or it should be purely phenomenological. Discussion of this question is frequently pre-empted by the words 'in our plural/multi-cultural/multi-faith (or, even) secular society . . .', without it being thought necessary to explain and justify this premise.

The theory underlying talk of 'the plural society' is flawed. Attempts to specify the basic minimum set of values which any society must have if it is to survive invariably fail. No doubt some sort of society could get by with very rudimentary standards of, for example, honesty and justice, but few of us would want to live in it. Most of the choices we have to make collectively are

about the sort of society we want to live in and bring up
our children in, and it is inevitable that, whatever choice
is made, some people will dissent from it. Thus,
changing patterns of family life are a matter of public
concern and even those who favour a variety of patterns
want to outlaw arrangements which involve gross
exploitation of women and children. This concept of
exploitation is sometimes interpreted in such a way as to
rule out anything like the traditional pattern of family
life which is regarded as inherently exploitative.
Similarly, the whole domain of crime and punishment
falls squarely within the public realm, but there are
deeply divergent views on what behaviour is to count as
criminal and what punishments are appropriate.

The fact that pluralism in its theoretical guise is
incoherent does not prevent its being a potent propa-
ganda weapon. It enables its proponents to disable the
opposition by depriving them of the right to influence
public policy while at the same time appearing themselves as the defenders and exemplars of toleration. In
fact, the toleration extended to religious bodies is
offered under a condition which they are unwilling to
accept, viz. that their activities should be limited to a
narrowly defined private sphere. Meanwhile, the positive
values adopted by those who advocate pluralism,
although powerfully advanced, are rendered effectively
invisible and immune to criticism.

The mainline churches have been slow to detect this
manoeuvre, and one is as likely to find the expression 'in
our plural and multicultural society' in a church
document as in a quality newspaper. It is not entirely
surprising, therefore, that the appeal to multiculturalism

has been seen most clearly for what it is by members of the Jewish and Muslim minorities. In a challenging paper, Mr Tariq Modood argues that, from the standpoint of religious minorities like Islam, an established church is preferable to a secular state. In developing his argument he draws upon the 1990 Reith Lectures by the Chief Rabbi, Dr Jonathan Sacks, whose theses he summarizes as follows:

(*a*) In the context of massive, but incomplete, secularization, the fate of all religions, minority and majority, hangs together;

(*b*) The effective maintenance of diversity requires that there also be an overarching public culture;

(*c*) If this public culture is to have any religious dimension it will be that of the premier religion, which for historical reasons in England is the Church of England, consequently all religious minorities ought to support it as a national institution.[3]

In terms of the argument I have been developing (*c*) asserts that the state cannot be morally neutral, and (*a*) and (*b*) assert that the choice for England is between a purely secular culture (in the guise of pluralism or multiculturalism) and one in which religion is able to play a part and which is predominantly Christian.

Both the Chief Rabbi and Dr Modood are in effect defending the constitutional position as it at present exists in England, and arguing that it should not be regarded as an obsolescent anomaly, nor allowed to

---

[3] Tariq Modood, 'Establishment, Multiculturalism & Citizenship', *The Political Quarterly*, 65, (1), Jan. 1994. Jonathan Sacks, *The Persistence of Faith*, The Reith Lectures (London: Weidenfeld and Nicolson, 1991).

decline into desuetude, but rather acknowledged and, where necessary, reformed.

For this proposal to be acceptable to religious minorities and to bona fide secularists, certain conditions are necessary:

(*a*) The Church must remain true to the Gospel it exists to proclaim. If it fails to do that, it will not be able to provide a firm framework of beliefs and values. An entirely progressive Church could not meet this requirement because it would lack independent authority. People turn to the Church, when they do, because they regard it as a repository of eternal truths which are not subject to the vagaries of fashion and are not merely human constructions. This is why it is often non-churchgoers who are most shocked when a bishop appears to deny the Resurrection or the parish church is found to have abandoned altogether the Prayer Book and the Authorized Version of the Bible. It is felt to be the Church's job to hold on to these things in case the individual should at any time need them. There is, of course, a good deal of unthinking nostalgia in all this, but it does also represent a conviction that the Church's teaching has no authority over men's minds unless it has a transcendent source of which these things are a potent symbol. This is why a radical theology which regards the Christian tradition as infinitely malleable, cannot meet their requirements.

(*b*) The Church must acknowledge its responsibility to the wider community by taking its problems seriously and seeking a Christian solution to them. Clearly there is a balance to be struck here. One sometimes hears it said that 'the world sets the agenda for the Church'. If

this were wholly the case, the Church would have
nothing distinctive to offer the world. But the Church
has a duty to help not only its own active members, but
those who turn to it from time to time in situations of
perplexity. And, if it is a national church, it has to go
beyond offering a Christian analysis of the problem and
suggest how it might be dealt with in practice, which
may often mean indicating what compromise with non-
Christian positions may be politically acceptable. In
point of fact the Church of England has a very
respectable record of this sort of activity in recent years
with its major reports on Faith in the Inner City and
Faith in the Countryside, as well as those on questions
of personal and social ethics produced under the aegis
of the Board for Social Responsibility.

The effectiveness of this work is often limited by the
way it is treated in the media. Journalists, whether in
television and radio or in the newspapers, have an
interest in confrontation which they assume is shared by
their readers and viewers. They are also attached to
stereotypes, so that developments which do not straightforwardly conform to stereotypes are either ignored
altogether or distorted so as to make them fit. Nor are
the stereotypes necessarily consistent. The Church, as
presented in the media, is hidebound by tradition and
out of touch with modern life; and, at one and the same
time, trendy and ambivalent and unable to make up its
mind.

(c) Both these requirements—that the Church should
remain true to the Gospel and that it should acknowledge
its responsibilities to the wider society—depend upon a
further one, which has been the main theme of this

book. It is essential that faith and criticism should be allowed to operate effectively in the life of the Church, and that the tension between them should be acknowledged freely by all parties. Misrepresentations in the media are lent some colour by the failure very often of traditionalists and progressives to recognize the role which each party has to play in maintaining a living tradition and in making it available to the world at large. In its relations with the secular world the Church must not abate its claims, but neither must it place itself above criticism or refuse to take account of the scientific discoveries and other movements of thought which both create many of our contemporary problems and may be needed for their solution. This is not simply a matter of learning the language of secular thought in order to make its message intelligible, but of striving to ensure that the authentic message of the Church is interpreted as fully and clearly as possible in the circumstances of the day.

(*d*) The Church should not expect that its values (and any specific recommendations based upon them) should *eo ipso* be mandatory upon a society which contains many groups and individuals who do not accept its premises. How far their influence extends is subject to the democratic process. But, given the need for a generally accepted public morality, there is no bar upon its being predominantly Christian. In practice, what emerges from the political process and from public debate about social issues will often be some sort of compromise within limits to be generally agreed and arrived at by procedures commonly accepted.

There are those who would argue that my first and

second requirements are incompatible. Any suggestion that the Church should accept the task of reinforcing to any extent the beliefs and practices of an existing national society and ministering to its needs, as it understands them, is inconsistent with the prophetic role of the Church, which must necessarily be in any society a challenging and disturbing presence.[4]

To this I would reply that the situation might come to demand the strict separation of church and state. Duncan Forrester instances the Confessing Church in Nazi Germany as a warning against the insidious effects of compromise upon a subservient Church. It is, indeed, an obligation upon the Church to indict the injustices of our own society, including those it inflicts upon others, and it could become so compromised as to be unable to do this effectively. But it is also incumbent upon the Church to support those institutions in society and those individuals who uphold and seek to maintain Christian standards where they are found in the actual working world. Such standards will only be exemplified imperfectly in any human community, including, of course, the Church itself. If the secular society is under judgement, so is the Church and it cannot, as an institution, claim to stand over against the secular society in pristine purity. In the Church's relations with society we have, in fact, a special case of the tension I have emphasized throughout. There are those whose job it is by temperament and vocation to ensure, so far as they can, that nothing is lost which has genuine

---

[4] See, e.g., Duncan Forrester's *Beliefs, Values, and Policies* (Oxford University Press, 1990).

Christian warrant and others whose role it is to criticize the status quo in terms of standards which better reflect the demands of the Gospel. Both parties are subject to temptations, to which they sometimes yield; traditionalists to complacency, progressives to self-righteousness. The pleasures to some temperaments of compulsive name-dropping are matched by the delight it gives others *'épater le bourgeois'*. Yet, however imperfectly they are realized, both emphases are needed.

The sort of society envisaged, which is by and large, though imperfectly, the sort of society we have, is best called a liberal society, i.e., one in which individuals and groups are able to follow their consciences within the framework of laws and other social arrangements which have been arrived at by processes in which they have been involved and, so far as possible, to which they have consented. It has often been remarked, and rightly, that a liberal society requires for its maintenance a comparatively high level of habitual good behaviour so that the law does not have to take too great a strain. Far from proceeding from a general scepticism about what is true and good of the sort that underlies the idea of the plural society, it requires to be based upon firm convictions about the worth of human beings and the respect due to them, and a reasoned trust in the capacity of men and women to recognize the truth when it is presented to them. A society cannot be a Christian society in any sense and at the same time a plural society in the fashionable sense of that term,[5] but there is no bar to its being a liberal society. For the convictions which

---

[5] The reference is to 'plural society' in sense (c) on p. 160.

underlie the liberal society themselves follow from a view of the world in which men and women have a worth in the sight of God which does not derive from the *de facto* attitudes of individuals or groups. As I have been concerned to argue throughout, whole-hearted commitment to thinking of men and women in this way is not incompatible with, but rather requires, fairness to opposing views and concern for those who hold them. Here too there must be faith; and there must be criticism.

INDEX